The Ultimate Guide to

Wonderful Wearables

by Barbara Finwall and Nancy Javier
BANAR DESIGNS, INC.

Meredith® Press, New York

Meredith® Press is an imprint of Meredith® Books

President, Book Group: Joseph J. Ward

Vice-President, Editorial Director: Elizabeth P. Rice

For Meredith® Press:

Executive Editor: Maryanne Bannon

Senior Editor: Carol Spier

Associate Editor: Ruth Weadock

Production Manager: Bill Rose

Cover Photograph: Julie Maris/Semel

For Barclay House Publishing:

Director: Barbara S. Machtiger

Designer: Robert E. Kiley

Copy Editor: Sydne Matus

For Banar Designs, Inc.:

Principals: Barbara Finwall, Nancy Javier, Arleen Bennett

Design Directors: Holly Witt, Barbara Finwall, Nancy Javier

Editorial Director: Jan Mollet Evans/MORE THAN WORDS

Designers: Barbara Finwall, Nancy Javier, Holly Witt, Patsy Needham, Sean Hancock, Nicki Birkett, and Susan Jones/JONES TONES

Painter: Winni Miller

Seamstresses: Nemie Torres, Marita Dionisio, Nicki Birkett, and Patsy Needham

Embroiderer: Nicki Birkett

Model Scheduling and Casting: Patsy Needham

Proofreaders: Holly Witt, Nemie Torres, Marita Dionisio

Photographers: William Ahrend Photography, Fallbrook, CA; Joni Prittie, Aptos, CA

Models: Paige Needham, David Shackelford, Megan Hill, Taylor Witt, Naomi Meza, Liz Opean, Holly Witt, Ben Cook, Linné Frame, Blake Turley, Nicole Turley, Stephanie Hintzaglou, Debbie Mirr, Julie Appleford

Staff: Yoshiko Ball, Tamiyo Dye, Cecil Ekrut, Jean Jarrell, Danny La Pointe, Liz Opean, Ayako Secola

ISBN: 0-696-20010-4
First Printing: 1994
Library of Congress Card Catalog Number: 93-08666-1

Published by Meredith® Press
Printed in the United States of America
10 9 8 7 6 5 4 3 2 1

Distributed by Meredith® Corporation, Des Moines, Iowa

Dedication

We'd like to dedicate this book to our mother,
Arleen (the AR in BANAR), who started it all.

—*Nancy and Barbara*

Dear Crafter:

Why is embellished clothing so much in vogue? Perhaps it's because all of us who enjoy crafting simply can't resist the opportunity to create—and wear—wardrobes that are truly personal. There have never been so many easy trimming and painting techniques available, or such a variety of designs to choose among. And you certainly don't need to be an artist or a fine seamstress to transform generic ready-to-wear (or recycled oldies) into one-of-a-kind fashions. So whether you love lace, ribbons, buttons, and beads; fusible appliqués or quickly painted motifs, a turn through these pages will inspire you to plan a closetful of wearables for yourself, your family, and all your friends.

In *The Ultimate Guide to Wonderful Wearables,* you'll find more than 65 charming, elegant, funky, and fantastic instant updates for all kinds of clothing, with styles ranging from an adorable collection of Kid Chic to a snappy Western Roundup of shirts, skirts, and vests. Choose splendid finery for nights on the town or casual togs for just knocking around.

To help you whip up an array of wearables, we've provided easy, complete, step-by-step instructions, full-size patterns, and full-page color photographs for every item. With these terrific trimming ideas, a few easy-to-find materials, and just a bit of spare time, you can create stylish, *wonderful wearables* that are as much fun to make as they are to wear.

Sincerely,

Carol Spier

Senior Editor

Contents

A Touch of Romance

Funky and Folky

For the Fun of It

Introduction

We were very excited when Meredith Press asked us to write this book. What a challenge— to design over 65 wearables using a wide variety of techniques and styles! Right away we decided that all the designs should be easy and quick to make. So, every garment in this book can be made in just an evening or two. We also wanted to create designs that would be inexpensive to make, with supplies that are readily available to all crafters. And, of course, we included designs for everyone in the family: Mom and Dad, teens, kids, and even babies.

The clothing and embellishments we used came from a variety of sources: discount stores for generic T-shirts and sweats; thrift shops and resale stores for vests and suit jackets; craft shops for aprons, hats, and trims; fabric shops for fabrics and trims; import stores for linens and doilies; and our own closets for dresses, blouses, and shirts in need of recycling. We even shopped at a hardware store and discovered some unique decorative accents. For your wearables creations, don't forget to look at garage sales and swap meets for antique linens, buttons, laces and trims. The Source List on page 165 will help you locate specific materials you can't find locally.

Before you start creating you own fashion masterpieces, here's a good tip. Sort through your closets, garage, laundry room, linen closet, and attic. Put all of the seemingly unusable clothes in a big rag bag. Don't throw any fabric items away; you can use them for everything from test swatches to cleanup rags for the inevitable messes. Save the treasures—embroidered linens, old buttons, costume jewelry, etc.— for use as embellishments. Keep an eye open for clothes that could use some artistic additions, perhaps to cover a stain or a tear. The items in your rag bag are great for experimentation before you actually paint, fuse, or dye a perfectly good item of clothing. Test your ironing technique on these old clothes before you fuse your first appliqué to a shirt. Try your hand with dimensional paints to learn how to avoid those pesky blobs and air bubbles. Examine paint colors and glitter effects, and perfect your rubber-stamping abilities.

Then get your whole family involved in creating their own outfits. We had some wonderful experiences when making assignments to our designers. Our teenage designers were more intrigued by the Funky and Folky projects, but Sean Hancock took a new approach to prom night and brought us his tie-dye tuxedo vest and bow tie (page 34), created to match his date's dress. The kids will love the cookie cutter designs; draw around them on fabric to create instant appliqués for holiday jammies (page 80). Our kids were proud of their oh-so-personal handprint appliquéd shirts (page 66), too. Let them help paint a Mr. Fix-It Apron (page 156) for Dad for a great Father's Day, Christmas, or birthday present. Dad can even get in on the fun by decorating his own shirts for that rugged individualist look.

We specifically designed the wearables in this book to inspire you to create your own personal designs, to improvise and become an accomplished wearables designer in your own right. Happy fusing, painting, gluing, and stitching!

The Ultimate Guide to

Wonderful Wearables

by Barbara Finwall and Nancy Javier
BANAR DESIGNS, INC.

General Crafting Information and Instructions

Preparing Garments and Fabrics

All washable garments, fabrics, and trims to be used in embellishing should be washed, dried, and pressed with an iron, if needed, before starting your project. Do not use fabric softener. Prewashing removes any sizing which may prevent paints, glues, and fusible webbing from adhering to the fabric properly. It also preshrinks fabrics. Of course, you should not machine-wash vintage fabrics, wool vests, lined jackets, or any fabric item marked "dry clean only."

Using Patterns

Many of the projects in this book have patterns supplied for cutting fabric appliqué shapes or for use as placement guides. You may copy the patterns for your own use either with tracing paper and a soft lead pencil with a rounded point or by photocopying. If an entire pattern is shown in the book, copy all the lines on your tracing paper or photocopy. If the pattern shows only half the design (half a heart, for example), fold the tracing paper or photocopy on the dotted line and cut through both layers to get the entire design when you open the paper.

After copying the pattern, you can often simply take your photocopy or tracing, pin it to the fabric, and cut out around the outside edges. If you do need to transfer the design to the fabric (for instance, if there is detailing inside the shape), you may use several means to do so; choose the one that best suits the project and your abilities:

Fabric marking pen with disappearing ink. This kind of pen allows you to trace around the outside of a pattern laid on the garment or to place a tracing underneath a light-colored garment and draw over the pattern lines that show through the fabric. A pencil can also be used, but fabric marker with disappearing ink has the advantage of fading away to leave a clean design.

Graphite paper *(also called transfer paper)*. Graphite paper is available in a variety of colors so you can choose the one that will show up best on your garment. Determine the placement of your design, hold or pin the tracing in place on one side, and gently slide the graphite paper under it, colored side down; redraw the pattern lines on the tracing paper, and they will be reproduced on the garment below.

Transfer pencil. This kind of pencil is used to transfer detailing after the pattern has been traced onto tracing paper with a regular pencil. Turn the tracing over and use the transfer pencil to redraw the pattern lines where they show through to the back of the tracing paper. This makes the design an iron-on transfer; when you turn it over onto the fabric and press it in place with an iron, the transfer pencil lines will appear on the fabric below.

Applying Appliqués

To attach fabric appliqués and other embellishments to garments, you may choose fusing, gluing, or hand-stitching techniques. Practice with the different techniques so you can discover the differences and advantages of each. Most of the projects give the preferred method for the materials being used; other projects allow you to choose the technique you are most comfortable with.

Fusing gives a smooth, regular appearance to fabric appliqués attached to garments; in most cases it is the preferred method of adhering appliqués. Fusing or hand stitching is better on lightweight materials, such as baby shirts, where glue may irritate the skin underneath. Hand stitching can give a more finished edge and is desirable when attaching only the edges of appliqués. Some materials work better with glue: it is preferred for attaching lace trims or doilies, for instance, or when you are working on very heavy or textured fabrics.

To Create Fusible Appliqués

Fusible webbing is a heat-set adhesive made into sheets that are covered with paper on both sides. Follow the manufacturer's directions supplied with the webbing. Peel the paper off only one side of the webbing, place the webbing paper-side up on the back of the fabric from which the appliqué is to be cut, and iron according to the manufacturer's directions. If there is a pattern, pin or trace it onto the right side of the fabric; many times there is no specific pattern, since the print on the fabric determines the appliqué shape. If you're making an appliqué from lace or crocheted fabric, place a piece of freezer paper over the fabric before ironing to protect the iron from the adhesive.

Using very sharp scissors, cut out the appliqué shape, leaving the paper backing on the appliqué. (*Note:* If the appliqué has interior detailing on the traced pattern, transfer those details at this point.) Position the appliqué on the garment, fabric side up, using the project photo or diagram as a guide; only when you have the final position determined should you remove the paper backing, replace the appliqué on the garment, cover it with a pressing cloth, and iron the appliqué in place.

To Glue Appliqués in Place

For use on clothing, glue must be washable. Check the label and follow the manufacturer's directions. If there is a pattern, pin or trace it onto the front of the fabric. Cut out the appliqué shape with very sharp scissors, using the pattern or the print of the fabric as your guide. Turn the appliqué right side down on your work surface, and run fine lines of glue crisscrossing the back of the shape. Use a straightedge, such as a small square of cardboard, to spread the glue thinly and evenly over the surface of the fabric shape. Hold the shape down on one side while you pull the glue toward the other edge; turn the shape around and continue to spread the glue until all the fabric, including the edges, is covered. Turn the appliqué over and hold it just above the garment until you determine the correct position. Lay the appliqué on the garment and smooth it into place with your fingers. Some projects call for only a line of glue around the edge of the appliqué. In that case, turn the appliqué face down, apply a thin glue line close to the edge of the appliqué, then turn it right side up and place it on the garment, pressing all the edges down with your fingers; wipe any excess glue off with a rag.

Jewel glue is specially formulated to attach rhinestones, jewels, pearls, cabochons, mirrors, etc. It dries clear and is washable and dry-cleanable. Follow the manufacturer's instructions for use and care.

To Hand-Stitch

Sometimes when working with delicate fabrics or baby clothes, a hand-stitched edge looks more finished. Determine whether you are going to be hand-stitching before cutting the appliqué, and if you are, add $\frac{1}{8}$"–$\frac{1}{4}$" to the size of the appliqué all around. Fold the edges of the appliqué back in a $\frac{1}{8}$"–$\frac{1}{4}$" hem, and topstitch by machine or lightly glue in place. Position the appliqué on the garment and pin it in place. Stitch around the appliqué, coming up from the back side of the garment, catching a few threads along the folded edge of the appliqué, and going back through the garment at almost the same place you came up; bring the needle up through the garment about $\frac{1}{8}$" farther around the shape, and repeat the process.

Using Dimensional Fabric Paint

To Seal Appliqué Edges

Fused appliqué—and sometimes glued appliqué—have raw edges. To keep the fabric from fraying and to stop the appliqué from coming off the garment, apply dimensional fabric paint around the edges. Dimensional fabric paint is an acrylic-based formula in a plastic applicator bottle with a fine tip; it is offered by many manufacturers in dozens of colors and finishes: shiny, metallic, pearlescent, iridescent,

and more. Choose the paint that will best complement your project, and follow the manufacturer's instructions concerning use and care. Be sure to store these paints upside down to allow all the paint to go to the tip, creating a freer flow of paint with fewer air bubbles. If the paint is clogged when you open it, insert a straight pin into the tip.

Practice painting on an old item of clothing or a piece of scrap fabric before you start on your project. You will get more comfortable with the feel of the paint bottle and achieve a nice, even, fine line. Use a paper towel to wipe excess paint off the applicator point as you work. Put the applicator tip where the raw edge of the appliqué meets the garment. Squeeze with even pressure, making sure the paint covers the edge of the appliqué and touches the garment. Turn the garment as you work to keep from smearing the paint you have already applied. If the project calls for glitter, sprinkle it on the paint while the paint is wet; for large designs, work in sections, so the paint will still be wet enough to hold the glitter.

Correct paint mistakes by sliding a sharp knife between the paint and the fabric and lifting off the paint; remove excess paint smears with nonacetone nail polish remover. If this isn't possible, add to the design to incorporate the mistake, making it look as if it were intentional. After you completely outline all the appliqué, leave the garment flat on your work surface and allow the paint to dry, following manufacturer's directions.

To Decorate

Dimensional paints can be used decoratively even when you are not sealing the edges of an appliqué. Use them to outline any shape or design feature you wish to highlight or to make dots (as on the Gem Tree Shirt, page 22), swirls, or accents. The Santa Fe Sunset Vest (page 14) is entirely embellished with dimensional painting. The vast array of finishes and colors is exciting and inspiring. Follow the instructions given for sealing appliqué edges (above) and practice to become comfortable with the application technique (dimensional paint is not applied or spread with a brush). Then let your creativity flow out of the tip of your paint bottle.

Using Acrylic Fabric Paint

Acrylic fabric paints are available in a huge range of colors, textures, and finishes. To paint on fabrics using acrylic paints, you must mix textile medium or extender with your paint. Follow the manufacturer's instructions for proportions and use.

Before painting, hand-wash your garment or wash it on the gentle cycle in hot water. Don't scrub, just lightly agitate. This removes sizing without raising the nap of the fabric too much. Hang or lay the garment flat to dry (don't use a dryer). Iron it if it has gotten wrinkled.

All outlining can be done using a liner brush. For larger areas, lay in the base color with a flat brush and lightly scrub the color into the fabric. Keep the color photograph of the project handy to refer to. To pat in the color, load a scrub brush with paint and tap off the excess onto a paper towel; then lightly tap the brush into the fabric. The brushes usually used for fabric painting are: a liner brush; flat #2, #4, and #8; and scrubber #2, #4, and #8.

When mixing colors, always start with the light color and slowly mix in the darker color until you have the desired intensity. If you have to hurry your drying time, a hair dryer works great.

Washing Your Embellished Garments

Generally, garments with embellishments glued or fused on or with dimensional paint added should be turned inside out for washing. Wash by hand or machine, following the garment manufacturer's guidelines. Allow to dry flat or on a line rather than in the dryer. An acrylic-fabric-painted garment can be washed by hand or on the gentle cycle of your machine. Wait 72 hours after painting before the first washing. Turn the garment inside out and use warm or cool water and mild detergent. Tumble dry on medium heat or lay it flat to dry.

Embroidery Stitching

Use an embroidery needle (sharp-pointed) for embroidery stitching. Floss is composed of six strands; use two to six strands, depending on how bold you want your stitching to be. Cut an 18" length of floss to work with at a time; it is best to prewash floss before using it to remove any excess dye, especially colors like red and black. An embroidery hoop should be used to hold fabric taut when embroidering. Use the colors and number of strands of floss indicated on the pattern for the project. Follow the diagrams provided here for each stitch to see just how it is formed. To begin, secure the floss to the back of the fabric with a small knot.

Blanket Stitch
Come up with your needle at **1** on the stitch diagram. Go in at **2**, leaving a small loop. Come up again at **3**, directly below **2** and in line with

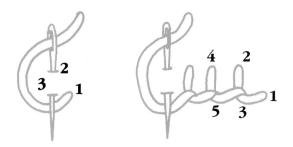

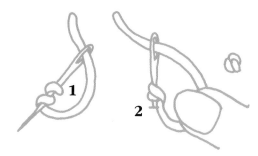

1, while holding the thread under the needle with your thumb. Pull thread through. Repeat.

Chain Stitch

Bring needle up at **1**. Form a loop and hold the thread down with your thumb. Go in again at **2**, next to **1**, and come up at **3**. Draw the needle over the loop. Don't pull the thread tight. Repeat, going down at **4** and up at **5**, forming a chain.

Feather Stitch

Come up at **1** and form a shallow loop. Hold the loop down with your thumb and go in at **2**. Come up at **3**, form a loop, hold it with your thumb, and go in at **4**. Continue, alternating loops side to side.

French Knot

Come up at **1**. Hold the needle close to the fabric and wrap the thread snugly around the needle two or three times. Insert the needle at **2**, very close to **1**, but not in the same hole. Keep the thread taut with your other hand while you pull the thread to the back of the fabric.

Herringbone Stitch

Come up at **1**. Go in at **2**, diagonally below **1**. Come up at **3**, level with **2**. Cross over the previous stitch and go in at **4**, level with **1**. Come up at **5**, level with **4**. Go in at **6**, level with **3** and **2**. Repeat.

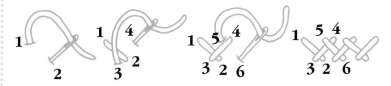

Lazy Daisy

Bring the needle up at **1**, make a loop with the thread, and hold it down. Go in at **2**, next to **1**, and come out again at **3**. Bring the needle and thread over the loop and tie it down with a tiny stitch at **4**. Then repeat for as many loops as you want.

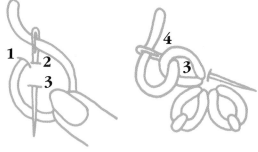

Satin Stitch

Come up at **1**. Go in at **2**. Come up again at **3**, very close to **1**. Go back in again at **4**, very close to **2**. Repeat, keeping your stitches smooth and even, side by side.

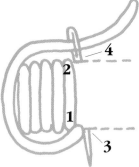

Daytime Glitz, Nighttime Glamour

For parties, dining out, or just plain fun, glitz is in. Transform ordinary street clothes into dazzling fashion statements with rhinestones, jewels, sequins, and glitter. Or create fabulous formal wear with techniques such as gold foiling, tie dying, sewing, and gluing.

Santa Fe Sunset Vest

Primary Technique: Dimensional Fabric Painting

Start With...

Vest with a Southwestern or Native American design (woven stripes, as you see on the one pictured, work particularly well); if you can't find a vest with a suitable print, get a solid black vest and use fusible webbing or fabric glue to add strips of colorful print fabric

And Add...

Dimensional fabric paints: with fine-line applicator tip, colors to match those in the fabric

Sprinkle glitter: Pastel and Aurora (source: Jones Tones)

From Your Craft Cupboard

T-shirt board or aluminum foil or waxed paper

Then Simply...

1. Avoid getting paint where you don't want it by using a T-shirt board or placing waxed paper or aluminum foil between the layers of the vest, covering the back of the vest where it is visible from the front.

2. Choose your paint palette to match the colors in the vest fabric. The design shown is formed entirely of horizontal lines. Trace over the design with the cool colors first, such as turquoise, purple, lavender, and green. Then sprinkle with Aurora glitter. Allow to dry; shake off excess glitter.

3. Paint the warm colors next: pink, orange, gold, bronze, etc. Sprinkle with Pastel glitter. Allow to dry; shake off excess glitter.

4. Leave black or open areas unpainted.

Sparkle Plenty

Left: **Sante Fe Sunset Vest**
Right: **Fruit Fantasy Tee**

Fruit Fantasy Tee

Primary Technique: Painting

Start With...

White T-shirt

And Add...

Fabric paints: Heavy Metal Liquid Glitter paint in green, purple, fuchsia, brown, and gold or yellow (source: DecoArt)

Textile extender or medium

Sequin strings: 1 yard green, 1 yard purple, ½ yard red, ½ yard gold, about 9" black (optional)

Painting patterns on page 17

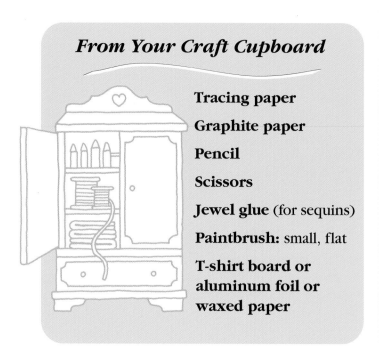

From Your Craft Cupboard

Tracing paper

Graphite paper

Pencil

Scissors

Jewel glue (for sequins)

Paintbrush: small, flat

T-shirt board or aluminum foil or waxed paper

Then Simply...

1. Use tracing paper and a pencil to trace the fruit painting patterns on opposite page. Put graphite paper under the tracing paper, colored side down, and position on the shirt, as shown in the photo. Trace all the shapes onto the shirt, moving the tracing and graphite paper as needed.

2. Following the painting instructions on page 11, paint in the areas of the design with flat color (no shading), using the photo as a color guide. Avoid the possibility of paint running from the front of the shirt to the back by using a T-shirt board or placing waxed paper or aluminum foil between the layers. Allow the paint to dry.

3. Use jewel glue to attach stringed sequins to outline one edge of the designs: green sequins along the green edge of the water-melon rind and the grape leaves, red along the fuchsia edge of the watermelon, purple along the edge of the grapes, and gold to outline the bananas. Cut nine 1"-long strips of purple or black sequins for the watermelon seeds, and glue 3 in place on the fuchsia part of each watermelon slice.

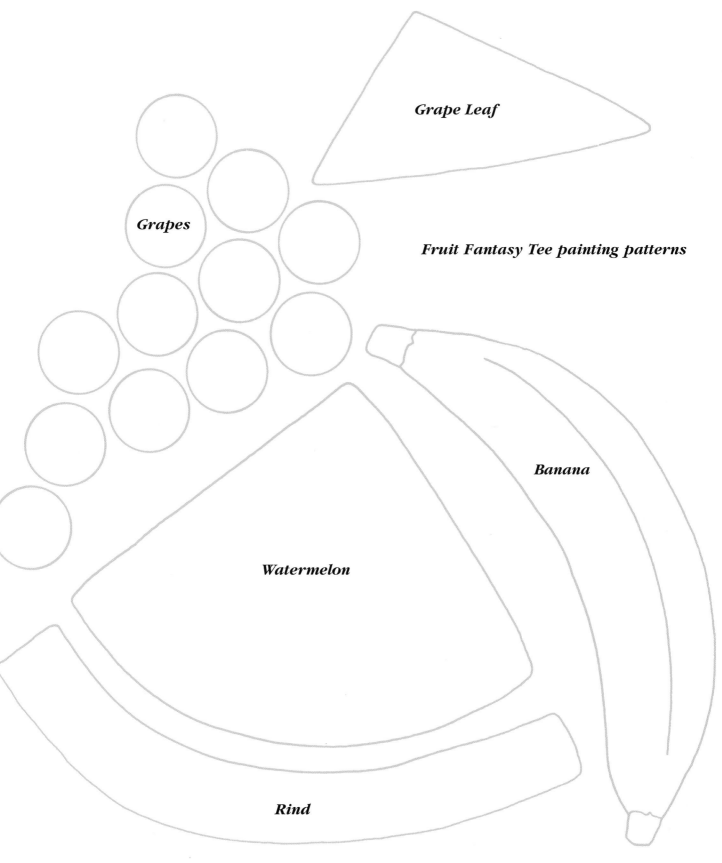

Grape Leaf

Grapes

Fruit Fantasy Tee painting patterns

Banana

Watermelon

Rind

Filigree Christmas Jacket

Primary Techniques: Fusing and Gluing

Start With...

White sweatshirt

And Add...

Battenberg lace trims: 3" wide, about 2½ yards (length depends on sweatshirt size), white (source: Peking Handicrafts)

Battenberg lace motifs: 2, about 5" x 9" each, white (source: Peking Handicrafts)

Fabrics: cotton/polyester blend, about ¼ yard each of burgundy red and hunter green

Sequins: about 36 each of red and green, ¼"

Fabric paint: white

Glitter: iridescent

Then Simply...

1. Place the sweatshirt on a T-shirt board or lay on a flat work surface. Find the center front of the shirt; draw a line down the front of the shirt, using a yardstick to be sure it is straight. Cut on that line to create an open-front jacket.

From Your Craft Cupboard

Fusible webbing

Freezer paper

Jewel glue (for sequins)

Yardstick and/or tape measure

Pencil or fabric marker

Scissors

Sewing machine and

notions or needle and white thread for hand stitching

Paintbrush: small, flat

Iron and pressing cloth or light towel (if using fusible webbing)

T-shirt board or aluminum foil or waxed paper

Glitter Wrap

Filigree Christmas Jacket

2. Cut the ribbing off the bottom of the sweatshirt and save it in your scrap bag. Make narrow hems on the bottom and front of the shirt by hand or machine.

3. Starting just below the neckline ribbing, measure the length down the front of the shirt and around the bottom to the center back; add 3" for overlap at the front corner. Cut 2 lengths of Battenberg lace trim that length.

4. Iron fusible webbing on the back of the red and green fabrics, following the fusing instructions on page 9. Cut a strip of red fabric and a strip of green fabric to the same width and length as the Battenberg lace trim.

5. Iron fusible webbing on the back of the Battenburg lace trim, placing a piece of freezer paper between the lace and the iron. Attach 1 of the lengths of Battenberg trim you cut in Step 3 to the red fabric and the other strip to the green fabric strip; both the trim and the fabrics should be right side up. Trim off the excess fabric around the lace. You will have 2 separate strips of fabric-backed trim: 1 of Battenberg lace backed with red fabric and 1 of Battenberg lace backed with green fabric.

6. Lay the red fabric-backed trim on the sweatshirt, starting just beneath the ribbing at the neckline and working down to the bottom of the shirt. Trim off the excess at the bottom (see Diagram 1-1), cutting around the curve of the Battenberg lace shapes. Fuse this piece to the shirt.

1-1

7. Cut the end of the remaining piece of red fabric-backed trim to fit around the bottom of the shirt, from the center back to the front, overlapping the end of the first piece you applied (see Diagram 1-1). Remember to cut all ends around the curve of the Battenberg lace shapes, not straight lines. Fuse in place on the shirt.

8. Repeat Steps 6 and 7 using the green fabric-backed trim.

9. Iron fusible webbing to the back of the Battenberg lace motifs, placing a piece of freezer paper between the lace and the

iron. Fuse 1 to a piece of the red fabric and the other to a piece of the green fabric; both the motifs and the fabrics should be right side up.

10. Fuse the fabric-backed lace motifs to the lower part of the shirt sleeves; the green motif should be on the side of the shirt with the red trim (applied previously) and the red motif on the side of the shirt with the green trim. If you see any areas that are not fused well, use washable fabric glue to firmly attach them to the shirt.

11. Brush fabric paint about $1/4$" wide on the shirt around the Battenberg lace trim and appliqués. Sprinkle glitter in the wet paint; allow to dry.

12. Glue the sequins over the trim down the front of the shirt and on the sleeves, using jewel glue and placing each sequin at the center of the shapes formed by the Battenberg lace. Place the red sequins on the green fabric-backed trim and the green sequins on the red fabric-backed trim.

Gem Tree Shirt

Primary Techniques: Gluing and Painting

Start With...

White sweatshirt

And Add...

Round gems: about 10 each in topaz, red, green, and dark fuchsia, 15 mm

Round gems: 6, 5 mm, crystal

Halogen glitter: fine, silver (source: Mark Enterprises)

Dimensional fabric paint: with fine-line applicator tip, white

Tree pattern on pages 24–25

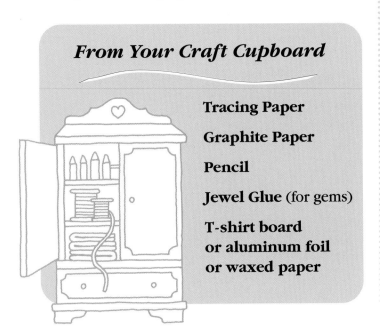

From Your Craft Cupboard

Tracing Paper

Graphite Paper

Pencil

Jewel Glue (for gems)

T-shirt board or aluminum foil or waxed paper

Then Simply...

1. Avoid adhering the front of the shirt to the back by using a T-shirt board or placing waxed paper or aluminum foil between the layers.

2. Use tracing paper and a pencil to trace the tree pattern on pages 24–25. Center the tracing on the shirt with the graphite paper beneath it, colored side down, and retrace to transfer the design.

3. Using the photo as a guide, glue on the gems. Allow to dry.

4. Paint the dot-pattern sunbursts around each gem with white dimensional fabric paint and sprinkle with glitter. Do not allow the paint to dry before adding glitter, so paint only about 4 gem areas at once, then glitter. Repeat until the entire design is complete.

5. Scatter 1/8" dots of paint about every 1/2" around the neckline and cuff ribbing and sprinkle on glitter. Allow to dry, then turn over and do the back of the neckline and cuffs with paint dots and glitter.

Christmas Lights
Gem Tree Shirt

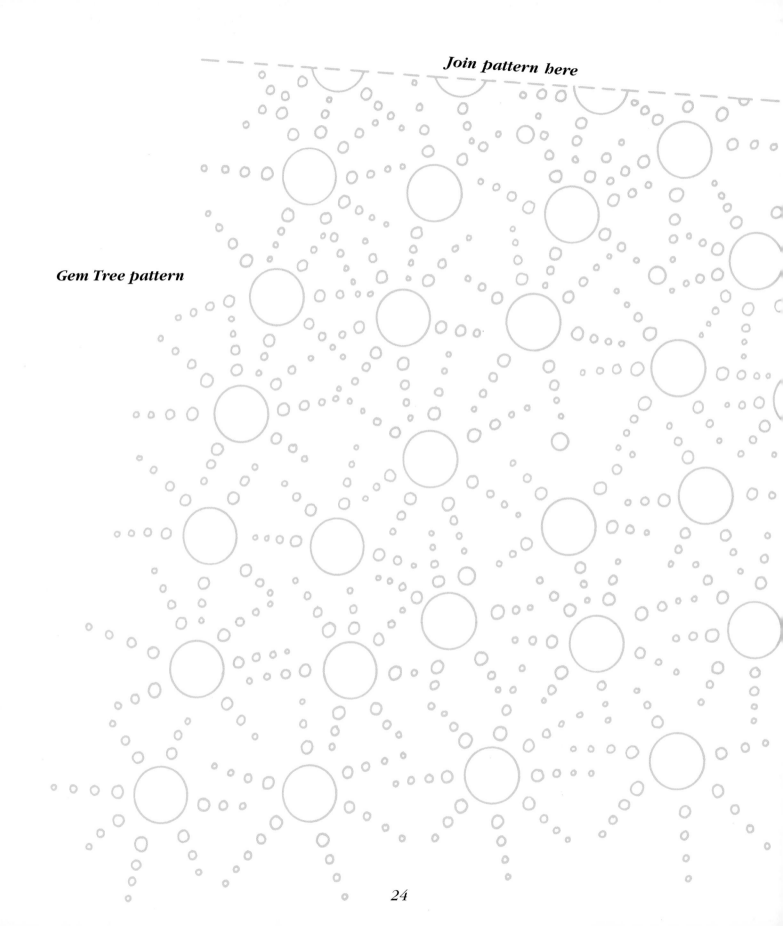

Join pattern here

Gem Tree pattern

24

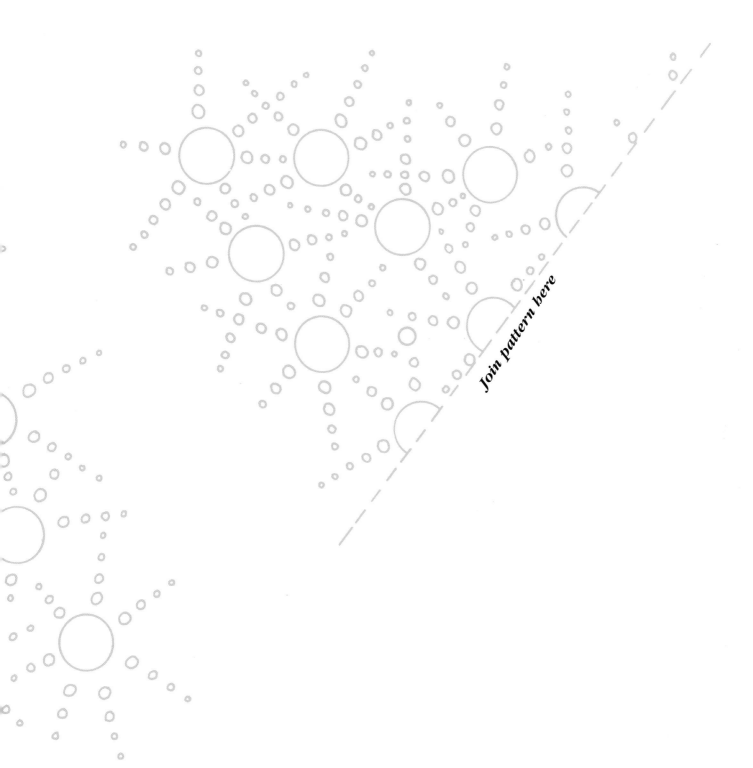

Join pattern here

Gold Lace Vest

Primary Techniques: Spray Painting and Gluing

Start With...

Solid black vest

And Add...

Lace fabric: ⅓ yard, gold

Sequin string: 3 yards, gold

Spray webbing: gold (source: Carnival Arts)

From Your Craft Cupboard

Scissors

Washable fabric glue (to attach lace cutouts)

Jewel glue (for sequins)

Craft knife (if vest has buttonholes)

T-shirt board or aluminum foil or waxed paper

Then Simply...

1. Avoid getting paint and spray webbing where you don't want it or gluing the front of the vest to the back by using a T-shirt board or placing waxed paper or aluminum foil between the layers, covering the back of the vest where it is visible from the front.

2. Spray the entire vest front with gold webbing, following the manufacturer's instructions on the spray can.

3. Cut floral motifs from the lace fabric and arrange them on the vest, using the photo as a guide. When the arrangement is pleasant, glue the lace florals to the vest front.

4. Outline some of the floral motifs with sequin string, using the jewel glue. Glue 2 or 3 sequins from the string to the middle of some of the florals.

5. If your vest has buttons and the holes have been covered by the lace, slit the lace carefully with a craft knife through the buttonhole from the back.

Midnight Flowers

Gold Lace Vest

Black Tie and Tuxedo Shirt

Primary Technique: Gluing

Start With...

White tuxedo shirt

Black long tie

And Add...

To the Tie:

Rhinestones (round): about 35, 4 mm; about 15, 6 mm; about 30, 15 mm; about 10, 22 mm; all white

Rhinestone stars: about 8, 7 mm, white

Rhinestone moon: 1, 15 mm, white

To the Shirt:

Rhinestones: about 60, 4-5 mm, white

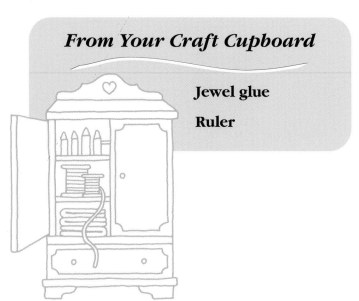

From Your Craft Cupboard

Jewel glue

Ruler

Then Simply...

For the Tie:

1. Glue the rhinestones to the tie, starting at the bottom and working your way up about 12". Use the photo as a guide. Start with the larger round stones first, scattering them around the tie. Then fill in a bit with the next smaller size, scattered over the tie. Keep filling in with the next smaller size stones, until the tie is almost full for about 12".

2. Add the moon about 13" up the tie from the bottom. Scatter the stars around it, leaving some space.

For the Shirt:

1. Glue 6 rhinestones in a triangular shape at each collar point.

2. Scatter the remaining rhinestones down the pleats of the shirt, gluing them on when you have a pleasant arrangement.

Cosmic
Dazzle

**Black Tie and
Tuxedo Shirt**

Golden Swirls Dress

Primary Technique: Gold Foiling

Start With...

Black sheath dress

And Add...

Rhinestones: about 60, 4–5 mm, clear

Liquid Beads™ Press and Peel Foil Beginner Kit (source: Plaid Enterprises)

From Your Craft Cupboard

Paper and pencil

Jewel glue (for rhinestones)

T-shirt board or aluminum foil or waxed paper

Then Simply...

1. Practice drawing swirling, curved shapes on paper. Refer to the photo for shape ideas. For best results the lines of your design should not be more than 1" apart.

2. Read and follow the manufacturer's instructions for using Liquid Beads foiling. Put the dress on a T-shirt board or lay aluminum foil or waxed paper between the layers to avoid adhering the front to the back of the dress. Apply Liquid Beads Dimensional Bond to create the swirling design on the upper part of the sheath, angling the bottom edge for a more dramatic effect. Allow the design to dry thoroughly.

3. Press on the foil using a stylus, following the manufacturer's directions, making sure the foil covers not only the tops but also the sides of the lines you have drawn with the bond. Apply the sealer.

4. Glue rhinestones in the center of each swirl formed by the foiling. Allow to dry.

Some Enchanted Evening

Left: **Golden Swirls Dress**
Right: **Shimmering Body Suit Formal**

Shimmering Body Suit Formal

Primary Technique: Sewing

Start With...

Black V-neck body suit

And Add...

Gold trim: 36" long (or hip measurement), about 2" wide

Gold V-shape appliqué: about 9" wide and high

Acetate fabric: 1⅓ yard (more for a longer skirt; 15" length shown here), black

Netting with gold dots: 1 yard (58"–60" wide), black

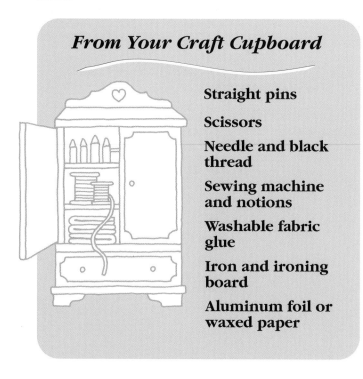

From Your Craft Cupboard

Straight pins

Scissors

Needle and black thread

Sewing machine and notions

Washable fabric glue

Iron and ironing board

Aluminum foil or waxed paper

Then Simply...

1. Lay the body suit flat and cut straight across the body suit at the hip (at the tops of the leg openings) to remove the panty portion.

2. For a skirt about 15" long from the dropped waist, cut the black acetate into two 18" x 45" rectangles (add or subtract length on the 18" side). Put the right sides of the acetate rectangles together, matching the sides and ends; pin and stitch a ¼" seam along one of the 18" ends. Open the rectangle, and run a gathering stitch along one 89½" side. Pull the gathering stitch until the length is the same as the hip measurement of the person the dress is for; knot the end of the gathering stitch. Fold the acetate in half so the 18" ends meet, with the right side of the fabric in; pin and stitch a ¼" seam along the 18" edge. Lay the fabric aside.

3. Cut 2 pieces of netting 15½" x 58" (or whatever the fabric width). Put the right sides of the netting rectangles together, matching the sides and ends; pin and stitch a ¼" seam along one of the 15½" ends. Open the rectangle, and run a gathering stitch along one 115½" side. Pull the gathering stitch until the length is the same as the hip measurement of the person the

dress is for; knot the end of the gathering stitch. Fold the netting in half so the 15½" ends meet, with the right side of the fabric in; pin and stitch a ¼" seam along the 15½" edge.

4. Put the net skirt inside the acetate skirt with both wrong sides facing out and the gathered ends aligned. The side seams should be aligned.

5. Put the body suit (right side out) inside the net skirt so the bottom of the body suit is even with the gathered edges of the net and acetate skirts. Pin the sides of the body suit to the side seams of the skirts by reaching into the bottom opening of the body suit you cut in Step 1. Pin the center front and the center back of the skirts to the body suit. Stretch the body suit as you go and pin about every inch to the gathered skirts; the body suit must be stretched enough to be the same size as the gathered skirts so it will go over the hip of the wearer. Machine-stitch a straight ¼" seam through both layers of the skirt and the body suit.

6. Pull the skirts down to hang beneath the body suit. Hem the acetate skirt, first turning up ¼" and machine-stitching, then turning up another 2" and hand-hemming. This should make the acetate and the net

skirts the same length; the net does not require hemming.

7. Glue the V-shaped appliqué just beneath the neck opening at the front of the body suit. Avoid adhering the front of the body suit to the back by placing aluminum foil or waxed paper between the layers.

8. Make a tie belt of the remaining black acetate. Cut 2 strips of acetate, each 45" long and 5" wide. Lay one on top of the other with the right sides in; pin and stitch a ¼" seam along the 5" side; open to form a 5" x 89½" rectangle. Fold this rectangle in half lengthwise with the right side in, to form a 2½" x 89½" strip. Stitch a ¼" seam along the 89½" open edge and down one 2½" end to the fold. Turn this strip right side out; push the open end into the tube about ¼" and whipstitch closed. Iron this tie belt flat. Cut the 2" gold trim to the length of the hip measurement; center it on the tie belt; each end will have some untrimmed black fabric, which will be knotted and form the ties that hang down beneath the belt.

9. With the dress on the wearer, tie the belt around the hips and pin at back center and on the sides. Remove dress and tack belt where pinned. Let the ties hang freely.

Tie-Dyed Bow Tie and Tuxedo Vest

Primary Technique: Dyeing

Start With...

White tuxedo vest and bow tie (available at tuxedo rental or sales shops, often at reduced rates for slightly stained items)

And Add...

Fabric dye: cold water type, choice of color (may match or coordinate with date's dress color)

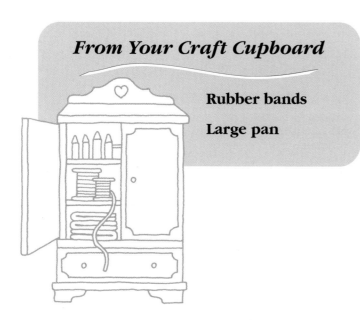

From Your Craft Cupboard

Rubber bands

Large pan

Then Simply...

1. Dampen the bow tie and the vest.

2. Place a rubber band around one end of the bow tie; twist it at the back of the tie and bring it around to the front again. Repeat until the whole rubber band has been used, spacing the wraps to allow about ⅛" of tie to show between them. Attach as many rubber bands to the tie as you wish; the more rubber bands used, the less dye color will be on the tie.

3. Gather up the fabric of the vest with your fingers, folding and crushing it as you go. Attach rubber bands in the same manner as you did on the tie.

4. Mix the dye according to the manufacturer's directions for pan dyeing. Submerge the tie and the vest in the dye. For very light color, leave in the dye only a few minutes; for more intense color, leave in the dye longer.

5. Remove the tie and vest from the dye and rinse under cold running water until the water runs clear.

6. Remove the rubber bands and reshape the tie and the vest. If a second color is desired, repeat steps 2 through 5.

7. After the tie and vest are dry, have them professionally dry-cleaned and pressed.

Prom Night

Left: **Tie-Dyed Bow Tie and Tuxedo Vest**
Right: **Posh Plaid Formal**

Posh Plaid Formal

Primary Technique: Sewing

Start With...

Crinkle stretch fabric: about 1/3 yard, black

Plaid taffeta: 1 1/2 yards (more for a longer skirt; 15" length shown here), 45" wide, black and white

Taffeta: 7" x 10", black

And Add...

Stretch lining (bathing suit fabric): about 1/3 yard, black

From Your Craft Cupboard

Straight pins

Scissors

Needle and black thread for hand stitching

Sewing machine and notions

Iron

Sequin trim: 2 2/3 yards

Snap closures: 2, large, black

Then Simply...

1. To make this dress, have the person it's being made for close at hand for frequent fittings. Take the 12" strip of stretch lining fabric and wrap it around the person to check for fit; pull it snug for a good fit. Mark the place where the fabric overlaps in the back with a straight pin. Cut the fabric 1/2" longer than your pin mark to allow for seam width. Take the strip of crinkle fabric and cut it to that same length. Fold the stretch lining fabric in half with the 12" ends together; machine-stitch a 1/4" seam down the 12" length. Turn this tube right side out and lay it aside. Fold the crinkle fabric in half with the right side in and the 12" sides together; machine-stitch a 1/4" seam down the 12" length.

2. Put the tube of stretch fabric inside the tube of crinkle fabric with the right sides together. Using a stretch stitch, stitch a 1/4" seam all along one end of the tube, attaching the lining to the crinkle fabric. This will be the top of the dress. Turn the tube right side out.

3. Try the tube top on the person. If it fits, continue; if not, adjust as needed.

4. Center the seam in the center back of the tube top, and find the center of the front. Use a needle and thread to gather both layers of fabric at the top of the center front; take a running stitch down from the top of the center front of the tube about 3"; pull the thread to gather the 3" length down to about 1". Tie the thread securely on the inside of the tube.

5. This step is easier if it is done while the top is being worn. Carefully pin the sequined trim onto the tube top, starting at the center back, going around the top of the tube, under the arm area, to within about 3" of the center front; then, leave the tube top and take the sequined trim over the shoulder to the opposite side in the back (so straps cross in back). When the trim meets the back, allow about 1" extra for a snap attachment and cut the excess off. Repeat the process for the other side of the trim. Remove the garment and stitch the sequined trim to the tube top. Leave each strap loose from the spot at which it leaves the tube top in the front to the cut end.

6. Pull the 2 snap closures apart. Stitch half of a snap closure to the sequined side of the trim about $1/2$" from the end of the strap; stitch the other half of the snap to the inside of the back of the tube top, about 3" from the center back. Repeat for the other strap.

7. For a skirt about 15" long, cut two 18" lengths of fabric the full 45" width of the plaid taffeta (add or subtract length on the 18" side). Put the right sides of the taffeta rectangles together, matching the sides and ends; pin and stitch a $1/4$" seam along one of the 18" ends. Open the rectangle, and run a gathering stitch along one $89^1/2$" side. Pull the gathering stitch until the length is the same as the bottom of the tube top, plus $1/2$"; knot the end of the gathering stitch. Fold the plaid taffeta in half so the 18" ends meet, with the right side of the fabric in; pin and stitch a $1/4$" seam along the 18" edge.

8. Put the tube top inside the taffeta skirt with the right sides of the fabric and the tube together and the bottom of the tube top even with the gathered edge of the skirt. The back seam of the top should be halfway between the two seams of the skirt. Pin the skirt to the top, stretching the top as you go. Machine-stitch a $1/4$" seam through the skirt and tube top. Pull the tube top from beneath the skirt, turning the skirt right side out as you go.

9. Topstitch sequined trim on where the top and skirt meet, starting and ending at the center back.

10. Hem the plaid skirt, first turning up $1/4$" and machine-stitching, then turning up another $1^1/2$" and hand-hemming.

11. Make 3 ribbon roses from the plaid taffeta. Cut 3 strips of fabric, each 6" x 24". Fold 1 strip in half lengthwise, with the right side in, to form a 3" x 24" rectangle. Stitch a $1/4$" seam along the open edge and down one 3"

end to the fold. Turn this strip right side out; push the open end into the tube about 1/4" and whipstitch closed. Iron flat. Repeat for the other 2 strips. Roll each strip of fabric into a rose: Starting at one end of a fabric strip, grasp the seamed side in one hand and turn until the entire length of the fabric is rolled up around itself; hand-stitch together at the bottom (seamed side), making sure the stitches go through all layers of the fabric so the rose doesn't come apart. Repeat for the other strips to form 3 roses.

12. Make a "leaf" bow from the black taffeta. Cut a 10" x 7" rectangle of fabric. Fold in half, with the right side of the fabric in, to form a 3 1/2" x 10" rectangle; pin and stitch a 1/4" seam along the 10" side. Turn right side out and iron flat. Bring the ends of the rectangle in to the center, pinching the ends and the center of the fabric rectangle together to form a bow shape; stitch in the center to hold the ends together and to keep the fabric gathered together at the center of the bow.

13. Stitch the leaf bow to the center front of the skirt, just beneath the sequined trim. Stitch the 3 ribbon roses in a group at the center of the leaf bow.

Western Roundup

Print fabrics, cowpoke appliqués, conchos, and Southwestern-style beads help create an authentic Western look. These fun Western wearables are sure to "round up" your wardrobe.

Decked-Out Denim Shirt

Primary Techniques: Fusing and Gluing

Start With...

Western-style denim shirt: with front yoke and flapped pockets

And Add...

Plaid flannel fabric: 1¼ yards, dark green and red-brown color

Heavy woven solid fabric: ¼ yard, dark green

Trim: suede-look, ⅛" x 60"

Then Simply...

1. If using fusible webbing, apply it to the back of all the fabrics, following the fusing instructions on page 9.

2. Lay the shirt on a flat work surface. Use tracing paper and a pencil to trace the shapes of the 2 pocket flaps and the 2 yokes—across the shoulder seam, down the arm opening, across the chest at the decorative seam, up the button placket, and around the collar to the shoulder seam. Mark right or left on each of the tracings to identify which side of the shirt the shape belongs on.

From Your Craft Cupboard

Fusible webbing or washable fabric glue (for fabrics)

Washable fabric glue (for trim)

Scissors   **Tracing paper**

Pencil   **Ruler**

Straight pins

Iron and pressing cloth or light towel (if using fusible webbing)

Craft knife (if shirt pocket has snap or button)

T-shirt board or aluminum foil or waxed paper (for gluing)

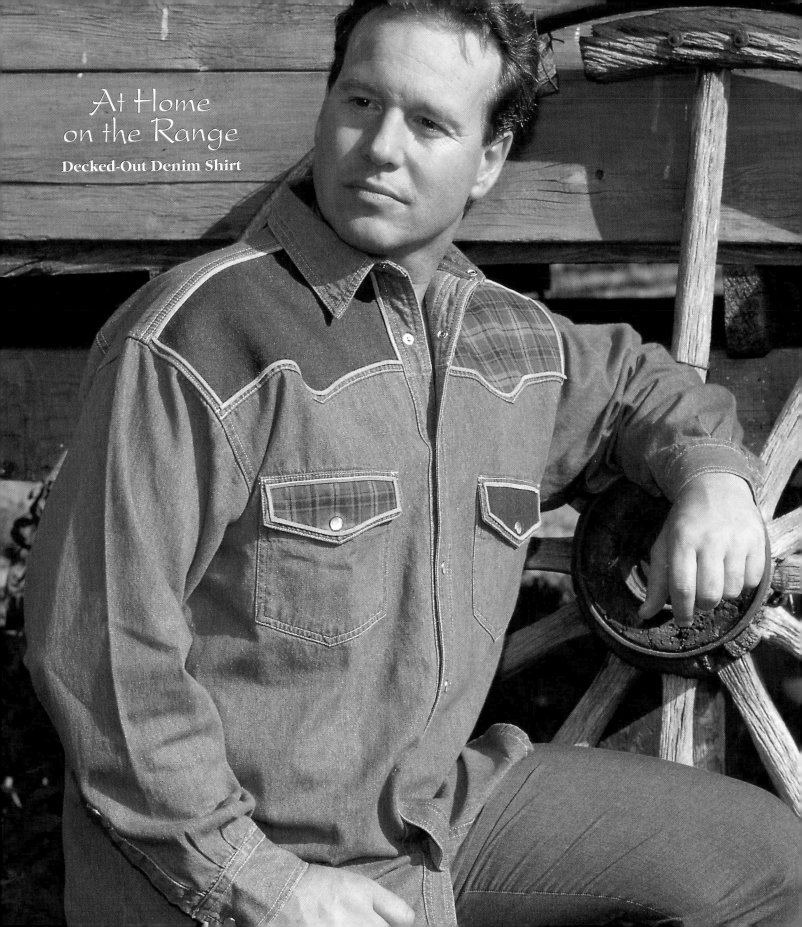

At Home
on the Range
Decked-Out Denim Shirt

3. Remove the tracing paper and lay the shirt flat on your work surface. Go over the tracing lines of the shapes, using a ruler to straighten them, if needed, and smoothing curved lines.

4. Pin the tracing paper for the right pocket flap and the left yoke to the plaid fabric and cut out the shapes. Pin the tracing paper for the left pocket flap and the right yoke to the solid fabric, and cut out the shapes.

5. Fuse or glue the fabric shapes in place on the shirt. If the pocket flaps have buttons, unbutton them before covering the flap with fabric. Avoid adhering the front of the shirt to the back by using a T-shirt board or placing waxed paper or aluminum foil between the layers.

6. If the shirt has snaps on the pocket flaps, use the point of the craft knife to cut through the material where it overlaps the snap covers. Cut the hole slightly smaller than the snap and push the fabric down under the edge of the snap cover. If the shirt has a buttonhole in the flap, turn the flap over after covering it with fabric and use the craft knife to cut the buttonhole through the fabric covering it. Be careful not to cut the fabric of the shirt.

7. Run a line of fabric glue around all the edges of one of the yokes, where the fabric meets the shirt. Lay the trim on the glue line, and press it down to hold it securely. Repeat for the other yoke and for the two pocket flaps.

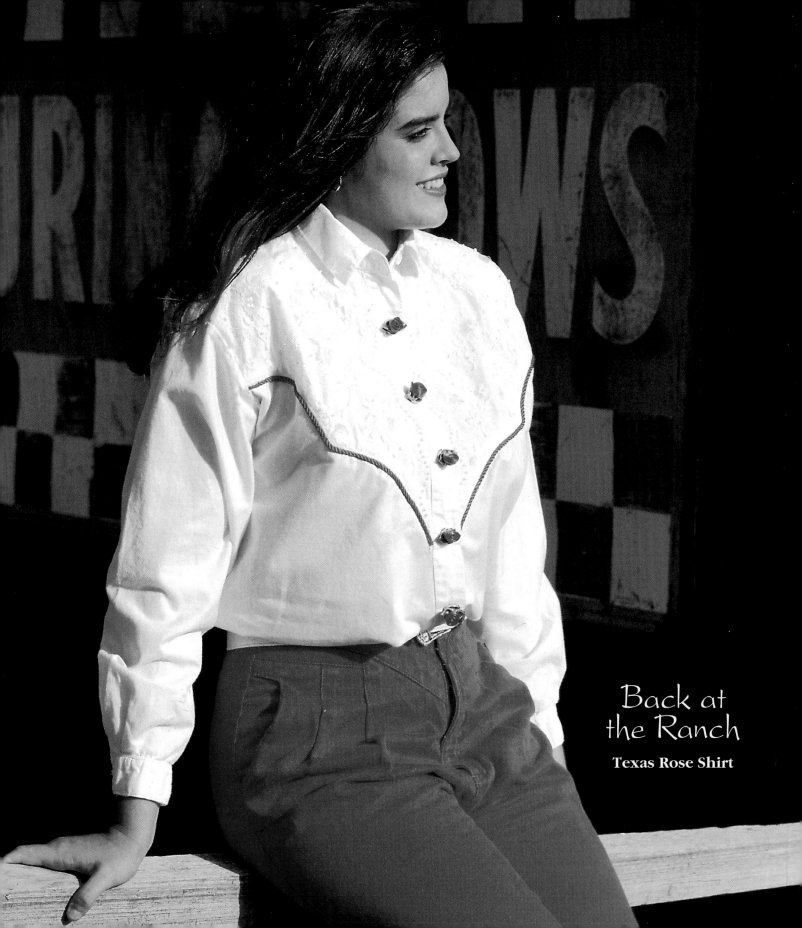

Back at
the Ranch

Texas Rose Shirt

Texas Rose Shirt

Primary Technique: Gluing

Start With...

Western-style white shirt: with long front yoke

And Add...

Lace fabric: 9" x 30" (with scallops along 30" length), white

Sequins: about 100, small, opalescent

Pearls: about 200, 4mm

Cording trim: ⅛" x 28", red

Button covers: 5 or 6 (to match number and size of shirt buttons)

Ribbon roses with ribbon leaves: 5 or 6 (number of buttons), large

Then Simply...

1. Lay the shirt on a flat work surface. Use tracing paper and a pencil to trace the shape of the yoke on one side of the shirt front—across the shoulder seam, down the arm opening, across the chest at the decorative seam, up the button placket, and around the collar to the shoulder seam.

2. Remove the tracing paper and lay the shirt flat on your work surface. Go over the tracing lines, using a ruler to straighten them, if needed, and smoothing curved lines.

3. Fold the lace fabric in half with the scalloped edges together to form a 9" x 15" rectangle. Pin the tracing paper with the yoke shape to the lace, with the

From Your Craft Cupboard

Washable fabric glue (for lace and cording)

Jewel glue (for sequins, pearls, and ribbon roses)

Scissors   **Tracing paper**

Pencil   **Ruler**

Straight pins

T-shirt board or aluminum foil or waxed paper

straight line representing the button placket along the scalloped edge of the lace; cut out along the other edges.

4. Run a thin line of fabric glue along the edge of the wrong side of 1 piece of lace. Turn over and press in place on the shirt. To make sure you put the glue on the correct side of the lace, lay the lace in position on the shirt, then turn it over onto your work surface and apply the glue. Avoid adhering the front of the shirt to the back by using a T-shirt board or placing waxed paper or aluminum foil between the layers. Repeat for the other piece of lace.

5. Run a thin line of fabric glue along the bottom edge of the yoke on one side of the shirt front, where the lace meets the shirt, from the armhole to the button placket. Lay the cording trim in the glue line, and press it down to hold it securely; cut off excess. Repeat for the other side of the yoke.

6. Use jewel glue to attach sequins in groups of 2-4 scattered over the lace.

7. Glue pearls every $1/2$" down the scalloped edge of the lace. Scatter additional pearls over the rest of the lace, in the centers of the floral motifs, for instance. Allow to dry.

8. Glue 1 ribbon rose to each button cover. Allow to dry. Slip button covers over buttons after the shirt is put on.

Cowgirl Jacket and Matching Skirt

Primary Techniques: Fusing and Sewing

Start With...

For the Jacket:

Denim jacket (source: Sunbelt Sportswear)

For the Skirt:

Plaid flannel fabric: ¾ yard, primarily red

Cow-print fabric: ⅞ yard

And Add...

To the Jacket:

Plaid flannel fabric: ¼ yard, primarily red

Cow-print fabric: ¼ yard

Dimensional fabric paint: with fine-line applicator tip, black

To the Skirt Fabric:

Flat waistband elastic that gathers with pull strings: 1½" wide, 60" long

Thread: color to coordinate with fabric

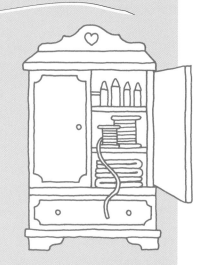

From Your Craft Cupboard

Fusible webbing or washable fabric glue

Tracing paper

Pencil   Ruler

Scissors

Straight pins

Sewing machine and notions

Needle and thread for hand stitching (basting)

Iron and pressing cloth or light towel (if using fusible webbing)

Then Simply...

For the Jacket:

1. Apply fusible webbing to the back of the ¼-yard pieces of the plaid flannel and cow-print fabrics, following the fusing instructions on page 9.

2. Lay the jacket on a flat work surface. Trace the pockets (not the flaps), the

In the Moo-d

Cowgirl Jacket and Matching Skirt

yokes, and the vertical strips below the pockets (between the seam lines) using tracing paper and pencil. Use the photo as a guide. Mark left or right on each of the tracings to identify which side of the jacket the shape belongs on.

3. Remove the tracing paper from the jacket. Use the ruler, as needed, to go over the straight lines to be sure they are absolutely straight; draw over the curved lines to make sure they are smooth around the armhole and neckline.

4. Pin the tracing paper for the left yoke and both vertical strips to the plaid fabric and cut out the shapes. Pin the tracing paper for the right yoke and both pockets to the cow fabric and cut out the shapes.

5. Fuse or glue the fabric shapes in place on the jacket. If gluing, avoid adhering the front of the jacket to the back by using a T-shirt board or placing waxed paper or aluminum foil between the layers.

6. Run a thin line of dimensional fabric paint around the shapes where they meet the jacket. Be sure the paint touches both the jacket and the edge of the fabric. This prevents fraying and loose edges.

For the Skirt:

1. Cut 2 pieces of plaid flannel fabric 13½" long and 30" wide. Lay one piece on top of the other, matching all the sides and with the right sides together. Pin across one 13½" end and stitch a ¼" seam on that end only. The finished strip will be about 59½" x 13½".

2. Lay the strip of flannel fabric on your work surface, right side down. Fold up and pin a ¼" hem along one 59½" side; stitch in place along the folded edge. Fold up that hem another 1", pin, and stitch in place by hand or machine. This is the hem of the flannel skirt to which the cow-print ruffle will be added.

3. Fold up the other 59½" edge, pin a ¼" hem, stitch in place along the raw edge. Fold up that hem another 1½", pin, and stitch in place. This is the waistband on which to stitch the elastic.

4. Lay the elastic over the waistband created in Step 3, starting at one end of the fabric strip and continuing to the other end, and pin in place. Following the directions provided with the elastic, straight-stitch on the blue lines of the elastic to attach it to the fabric. Pull the strings at one end of the elastic to gather it to about 4" smaller than the waist measurement of the person you are making the skirt for.

5. Fold the flannel fabric in half, right side in, with the two raw edges together. Pin in place and stitch a ¼" seam through both layers of the fabric and the elastic. Cut off the excess strings you pulled from the elastic to gather it. Lay the flannel skirt aside.

6. Cut the cow-print fabric into three 10" strips across the full 45" width of the fabric. Lay one of the strips on top of the other, matching all the sides and with the right sides together. Pin across one 10" end, and stitch a ½" seam on that end only. Open the strip up; it is now approximately 89½" long by 10" wide. Lay another strip over one end of the 89½" long strip, with the right sides together; pin, seam across the 10" end, and open the strip up. The finished strip will be 134" long by 10" wide. Pin the two 10" ends together, right side in, and seam together to form a loop.

7. Fold up and pin a ¼" hem in the bottom of the cow-print ruffle; stitch in place along the folded edge. Fold up that hem another 1", pin, and stitch in place by hand or machine. This makes the cow print ruffle about 8" long.

8. Run a gathering stitch along raw edge of the cow-print loop. Pull the thread until the length of the gathered edge matches the length along the bottom edge of the flannel skirt. Align the gathered edge of the cow-print ruffle with the hemline of the skirt with right sides together. Pin, and then stitch a ¼" seam, joining the two. Turn the skirt right side out.

Decorated Denim Appliquéd Shirt

Primary Techniques: Gluing and Embroidery

Start With...

Sleeveless chambray shirt

And Add...

Iron-on appliqués with a Western theme:
4, about 2" across; boots, hat, saddle, star, etc.

Embroidery floss: brown

Then Simply...

1. Iron the appliqués onto the yoke and pockets of the shirt, using the photo as a guide.

2. Following the embroidery instructions on page 11, blanket-stitch over the yoke seams and around the edge of the collar of the shirt.

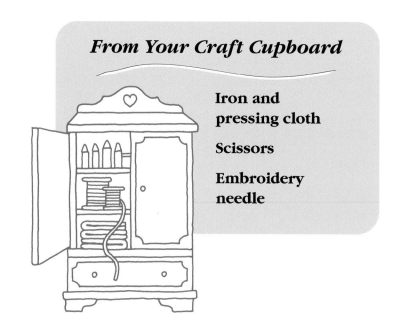

From Your Craft Cupboard

Iron and pressing cloth

Scissors

Embroidery needle

Howdy, Pardner

Decorated Denim
Appliquéd Shirt

Broomstick Skirt and Matching Top

Primary Technique: Sewing

Start With...

Western print fabrics: 3 different prints
(⅝ yard for the top ruffle, 1 yard for the middle
ruffle, and 1⅓ yards for the bottom ruffle); this
makes a skirt approximately 22" long—for a
longer skirt, add additional ruffles or make each
of the three ruffles longer; 100% cotton, 45" wide

T-shirt: V-neck, short-sleeve, black

And Add...

For the Skirt:

**Flat waistband elastic that gathers with
pull strings:** 1½" wide, 90" long

Thread: color to coordinate with fabric

For the Shirt:

Conchos: 3, approximately 1¼" across, stars
or other Western motif, silver

Fabric scraps from skirt: 3, ½" x 8" strips

Beads: 6 hearts, about 10 mm, and 6 pony
beads, about 10 mm, colors to coordinate
with fabrics

Thread: color that contrasts with shirt and
coordinates with skirt

From Your Craft Cupboard

**Fabric marker or
pencil**

Scissors

Straight pins

**Sewing machine
and notions**

**Needle and thread
for hand stitching**
(attaching conchos)

Then Simply...

For the Skirt:

1. Cut the fabric in strips across the full 45"
width of the fabric. The top ruffle will be
made from 2 strips, each 11" wide. The
middle ruffle is 4 strips, each 8" wide. The
bottom ruffle is 5 strips, each 9½" wide
(to allow for 1½" hem). If you wish to add
a fourth ruffle, make the third ruffle (for-
merly the bottom ruffle) 8" wide; then cut
the fourth ruffle of 6 strips 9½" wide.

Saturday Night Special

Broomstick Skirt and Matching Top

2. Lay one of the 2 strips of fabric for the top ruffle, on top of the other, matching all the sides and with the right sides together. Pin across one 11" end, and stitch a $\frac{1}{4}$" seam on that end only. The finished strip will be about 89$\frac{1}{2}$" x 11". Lay aside.

3. Put the right sides of 2 of the strips for the middle ruffle together, as you did in Step 2. Pin and seam across the 8" end. Open the strip up; it is now 89$\frac{1}{2}$" long by 8" wide. Lay another strip over one end of the 89$\frac{1}{2}$" long strip, with the right sides together; pin, seam across the 8" end, and open the strip up. Repeat to add the fourth strip. The finished strip for the middle ruffle will be about 178$\frac{1}{2}$" long by 8" wide. Pin the two 8" ends together, right side in, and seam together to form a loop. Lay aside.

4. Seam together the 5 pieces for the bottom ruffle, as you did for the middle ruffle in Step 3. The finished strip for the bottom ruffle will be 223" long by 8" wide. Pin the two 8" ends together, right side in, and seam together to form a loop. Lay aside.

5. Lay the strip for the top ruffle on your work surface, right side down. Fold down and pin a $\frac{1}{4}$" hem along one 89$\frac{1}{2}$" side; stitch in place along the raw edge. Fold down that hem another 2", pin, and stitch in place. This is the waistband on which to stitch the elastic.

6. Lay the elastic over the waistband created in Step 5, starting at one end of the strip and continuing to the other end, and pin in

place. Following the directions provided with the elastic, straight-stitch on the blue lines of the elastic to attach it to the fabric beneath it. Pull the strings at one end of the elastic to gather it to about 4" smaller than the waist measurement of the person you are making the skirt for.

7. Fold the ruffled fabric in half, right side in, with the two 11" ends together. Pin in place and stitch a $\frac{1}{4}$" seam down the 11" edge, through both layers of the fabric and the elastic. Cut off the excess strings you pulled from the elastic to gather it.

8. To add the remaining ruffle pieces, run a gathering stitch along one edge of the loop created for the middle ruffle. Pull the thread until the length of the gathered edge matches the length along the bottom edge of the top ruffle. Pin the gathered edge to the bottom edge of the top ruffle, with the right sides of the fabric together. Stitch to attach with a $\frac{1}{4}$" seam. Repeat with the bottom ruffle, gathering it to the length of the bottom of the middle ruffle. Hem the bottom of the skirt: fold in $\frac{1}{4}$", stitch, then fold in 1$\frac{1}{2}$", and hem by hand or machine.

9. To get the wrinkled look that characterizes the broomstick skirt, women used to wrap their skirt around a broomstick when the skirt was wet from washing, then tie it in place until it was dry—therefore, the name "broomstick" skirt. Nowadays, the method is much easier. Cut the foot out of a nylon stocking; pull the nylon onto your arm, with your hand sticking out one end. Take your

skirt damp from the washing machine (after all cycles are complete), bunch the waistband elastic together, and grasp the elastic in one hand (the same arm you have the nylon on). Use your other hand to pull the nylon down over the entire skirt, rotating the hand holding the waistband to twist the fabric; this bunches the skirt to form the wrinkles. Release the skirt, and pull your hand out of the nylon. Let the skirt dry fully in the nylon; remove only when you are ready to wear it.

For the Shirt:

1. Cut 3 strips of fabric, each about ½" x 8".

2. Run a strip of fabric through one concho; pull through evenly so two 4" lengths are hanging to the front of the concho. Tie an overhand knot to hold the fabric to the concho.

3. Put 1 heart bead and 1 pony bead on each length of fabric; tie a knot in each end to keep the beads from sliding off.

4. Repeat for the other 2 conchos.

5. Hand-stitch the conchos to the shirt front, using the photo as a guide. Stitch through the fabric only where it comes through the back of the concho; let the bead strings hang free.

6. Give the neckline and sleeves a ruffled look ("lettuce" edging) using red thread or another contrasting color that coordinates with the skirt fabric. Use a tight zigzag stitch on your sewing machine or serger at the outer edge of the ribbing; stretch the fabric by pulling it taut as you stitch for maximum ruffling.

Felt Appliquéd Vest

Primary Technique: Fusing or Gluing

Start With...

Black felt: 24" x 48" (or a black vest)

And Add...

Felt: about 6" squares of each color: red, green, purple, yellow, black, brown, beige

Washers: 3, 1", silver color

Studs: 4, 5 mm, silver color

Bugle beads: 24, iridescent red

Rickrack: wide, about 4 yards, red

Fringe: about 3" long, 1⅓ yards, red

Embroidery floss: red, green, yellow, lavender

Vest pattern on pages 62–63

Appliqué patterns on pages 60–61

Then Simply...

1. Use tracing paper and a pencil to trace the pattern for the vest neck, shoulder, and armhole on pages 62-63.

2. Lay the black felt on your work surface. Fold each of the 24" ends in toward the center of the 48" length so the ends meet in the middle; this will make a 24" square. Pin

From Your Craft Cupboard

Tracing paper

Pencil   **White chalk**

Ruler or yardstick

Scissors   **Straight pins**

Embroidery needle

Fusible webbing or washable fabric glue (to attach fabric cutouts)

Washable fabric glue (to attach trim)

Iron and pressing cloth or light towel (if using fusible webbing)

T-shirt board or aluminum foil or waxed paper (if gluing)

Fringe Benefits
Felt Appliquéd Vest

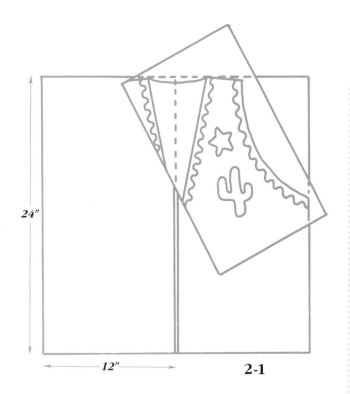

2-1

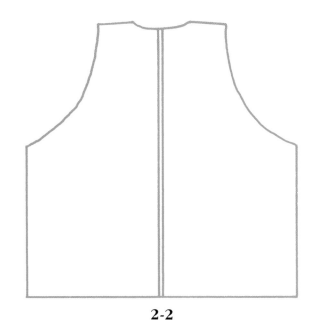

2-2

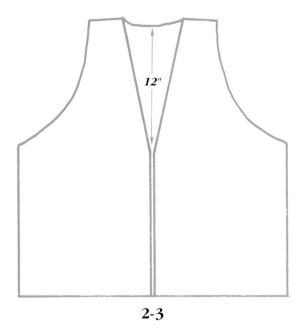

2-3

the tracing on one side of the felt with the bottom of the armhole at the folded edge and the point at which the shoulder seam meets the neckline at the top, open edge of the felt; cut out the armhole, shoulder, and back neckline, cutting through both layers of the felt (see Diagram 2-1). Unpin the tracing from the felt and turn it over to use on the other side of the vest; pin as you did before with the bottom of the armhole at the folded edge and the point at which the shoulder meets the neckline at the top, open edge of the felt. Cut the armhole, shoulder, and back neckline, then remove the tracing paper (see Diagram 2-2).

3. Measure and mark where you will cut the front neck opening of the vest (see Diagram 2-3). Start in the center front where the two sides of the felt meet; measure 12" down from the back neckline and make a mark with the chalk on both sides of the center opening. On both sides of the vest front, draw a line from that mark to the point at which the shoulder meets the back neckline. Cut through the top layer of fabric only, and lay the scraps aside.

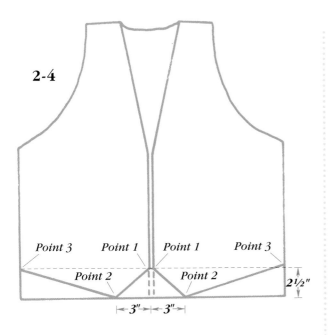

2-4

Point 3　Point 1　Point 1　Point 3

Point 2　Point 2

2½"

|←3"→|←3"→|

the bottom of the felt 3" from the center where the two sides of the felt meet; mark on both the right and left sides of the vest front (points 2). Measure 2½" up the folded edge and mark on both the right and left sides (points 3). Draw a line connecting points 1, 2, and 3 on each side of the vest front; cut on the line through the top layer of fabric only.

5. Open the vest front, and lay the felt flat on your work surface. Draw a line straight across the back, connecting point 3 on the left with point 3 on the right (see Diagram 2-5). Cut this 2½" strip off the back of the vest.

4. Measure and mark the bottom of the vest (see Diagram 2-4). Start in the center front where the two sides of the felt meet; measure 2½" up from the bottom and make a mark with the chalk on both sides of the center opening (points 1). Measure across

6. Trace the patterns on pages 60–61 for the Western-shape appliqués. If using fusible webbing, follow manufacturer's instructions and fuse to felt before cutting out appliqué shapes. Cut the shapes out of

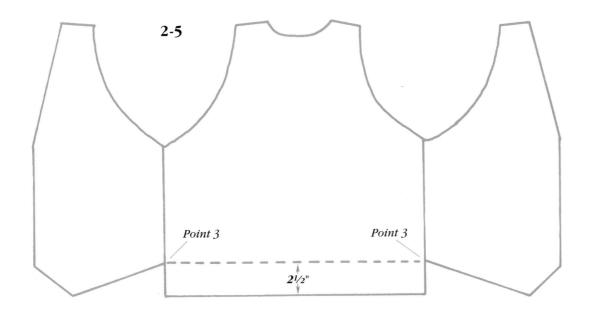

2-5

Point 3　　　　Point 3

2½"

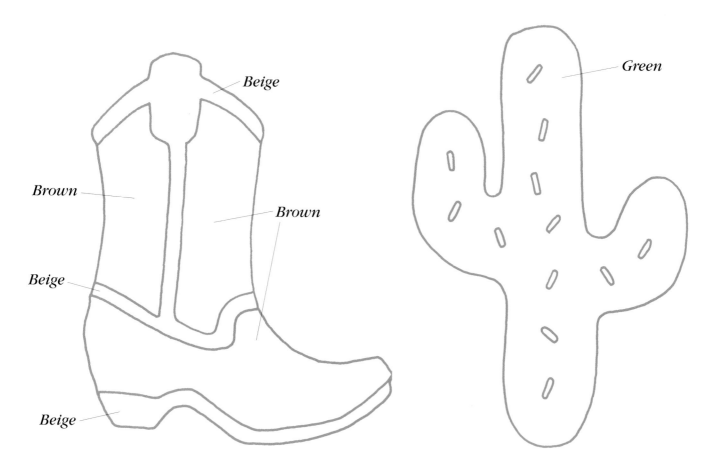

Beige

Brown

Brown

Beige

Beige

Green

Felt Appliquéd Vest patterns

felt: 3 purple stars, 4 red hearts, 2 green cacti, 2 beige boots, 2 brown boot details, and 1 yellow arrowhead.

7. Use green embroidery floss to stitch 12 of the bugle beads randomly on each cactus to represent thorns.

8. Glue the brown shapes onto the beige boots. Glue the hearts in the centers of the arrowhead and stars. Using the photo as a guide, position the felt shapes on the vest front.

Following the fusing or gluing instructions on page 9, fuse or glue the appliqués. Avoid adhering the front of the vest to the back by using a T-shirt board or placing waxed paper or aluminum foil between the layers.

9. Push the studs through the centers of the hearts on the stars and the arrowhead and down through 1 layer of the vest. Flatten the points toward the center on the back to attach them securely.

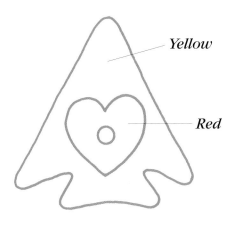

Yellow

Red

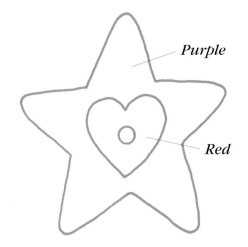

Purple

Red

10. Overlap the shoulder seams about ¼" and glue the front to the back at each shoulder. Allow to dry.

11. Following the embroidery instructions on page 11, blanket-stitch with the red floss around the outside edge of all the felt shapes you glued on. Blanket-stitch over the shoulder seam you glued.

12. Scatter the washers on the vest (see photo), and use 6 strands of the floss to stitch them in place with about 4 stitches in a sunburst pattern, from the inside to the outside of the washer.

13. Glue rickrack around the neckline, down the front, and around the bottom of the vest. Also glue rickrack around the armholes.

14. Glue fringe along the bottom of the vest; the top of the fringe should be glued just under the edge of the felt.

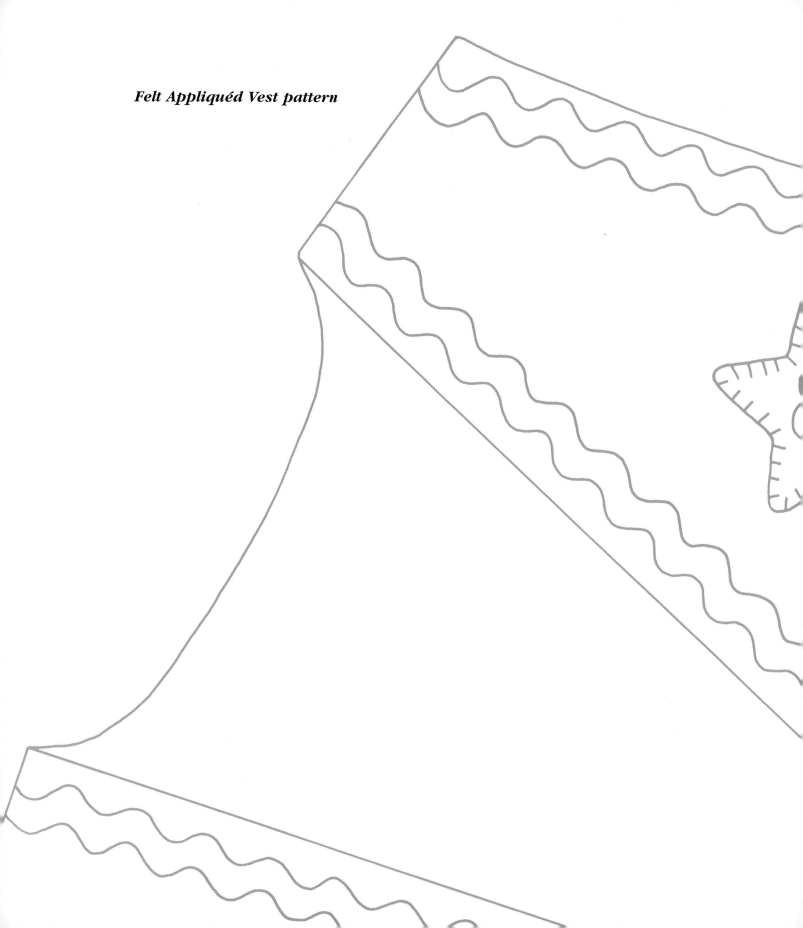

Felt Appliquéd Vest pattern

Kid Chic

Whimsical clothing accents for the little ones can be found almost anywhere. Your linen closet, attic, and kitchen hold treasures that can provide charming embellishments. Even the kids can be a resource, as the handprint shirts in this chapter will attest.

Lend a Hand

**Handprint Shirts and
Matching Shoes**

Handprint Shirts and Matching Shoes

Primary Technique: Fusing or Gluing

Start With...

Child-size T-shirt

Canvas shoes with shoelaces

And Add...

To the Shirts:

Fabrics appropriate for the child: 4 pieces about 6" square; we used pink and white stripes, and mint green and white checks on one shirt; black and white prints with stars, checks, stripes, and dots on the other. To add a ruffle to the bottom of your shirt, add about 2" x 45" of one of the fabrics

Ribbon roses with leaves: 4, small, in colors to coordinate with fabrics (optional)

Dimensional fabric paint: with fine-line applicator tip, color to coordinate with fabrics

Small heart pattern on page 67

To the Shoes:

Fabrics to match shirt decorations: ½" x about 45" for each pair of shoes

Ribbon roses with leaves: 2, small, in colors to coordinate with fabrics (optional)

Dimensional fabric paint: with fine-line applicator tip, color to coordinate with fabrics

From Your Craft Cupboard

Fabric marker with disappearing ink or pencil

Scissors

Fusible webbing or washable fabric glue (to attach hand-prints and hearts)

Washable fabric glue (to attach ribbon roses, if desired)

Sewing machine and notions or needle and thread for hand stitching (if adding ruffle)

Iron and pressing cloth or light towel (if using fusible webbing)

Aluminum foil or waxed paper (if gluing)

Clear tape: ½" wide (for shoelaces)

Then Simply...

For the Shirts:

1. If you are using fusible webbing, iron it on the back of the fabric squares, following the fusing instructions on page 9.

2. Lay the fabric right side up on your work surface. Use a pencil or fabric pen to trace the child's right hand on 2 of the fabric squares and her or his left hand on the other 2 squares. Trace the heart pattern, below, beside the hands on each of the fabric squares. Cut out the 4 hands and 4 hearts.

3. If you are using fusible webbing, lay the hands on the front of the T-shirt, placing the right hands on the right side and left hands on the left side, as you face the shirt. Put a fabric heart in the center of each fabric hand; be sure to use a heart from a different fabric than the hand is made of. Iron each hand in place, attaching the hand to the shirt and the heart to the hand at the same time.

***Handprint Shirt and Shoes
heart appliqué pattern***

4. If you are using fabric glue to attach the hands to the shirt, place the hands on the shirt with the right hands on the right side and the left hands on the left side as you face the shirt. Glue the hands to the shirt, then glue a heart in the center of each hand. Avoid adhering the front of the shirt to the back by placing waxed paper or aluminum foil between the layers of the shirt.

5. Run a thin line of dimensional fabric paint around the hands where the hand fabric meets the shirt and around the hearts where the two fabrics meet (see the photo). This prevents fraying and loose edges.

6. Glue ribbon roses in the centers of the hearts, if desired.

7. If you want to give the neckline and sleeves a ruffled look ("lettuce" edging), use a tight zigzag stitch on your sewing machine or serger at the outer edge of the ribbing; stretch the fabric by pulling it taut as you stitch for maximum ruffling.

8. To add a ruffle of fabric at the bottom of the shirt, cut a 2" x 45" length of one of the heart fabrics. Machine-overcast one edge of the strip. Run a gathering stitch, by machine or hand, along the opposite side, about ¼" down from the raw edge of the fabric; pull the thread to gather the strip to the length of the bottom of the shirt, stretched to its maximum. Put the ends of the strip together, with right side of the fabric to the inside, and make a ¼" seam on the end. Align the gathered edge of the ruffle with the bottom of the shirt, right sides together, stretching the shirt as you go. Pin, starting at the seam in the ruffle, having placed it at the center of the back of the shirt. Stitch the ruffle onto the shirt, making a ¼" seam.

For the Shoes:

1. Remove the shoelaces from a pair of shoes and measure the length.

2. Cut two ½"-wide strips of fabric to coordinate with the shirt; cut the fabric strips to the length of the shoelace.

3. Twist the end of one fabric strip, and roll tape around it tightly to form the shoelace tip. Repeat for the other ends. Lace into the shoes.

4. Cut hearts, if desired, and glue to the shoes. Run a thin line of dimensional fabric paint around the hearts, making sure the paint touches both the shoe and the edge of the heart fabric. Glue a ribbon rose to the center of the heart, if desired.

Pick a Peck
of Patches

Colorful Patched Overalls

Colorful Patched Overalls

Primary Techniques: Fusing and Gluing

Start With...

Child-size overalls

And Add...

Fabric scraps: various colors (red, teal, purple, blue, etc.)

Rickrack: baby size, 14", yellow

Buttons: about 7, ³⁄₈"–¹⁄₂", various colors to coordinate with fabrics

Then Simply...

1. If using fusible webbing, apply it to the back of all the fabrics, following the instructions on page 9.

2. Lay the overalls on a flat work surface. Place tracing paper over the large pocket on the bib of the overalls and use a pencil to trace the shape just inside the seam. Pin the tracing to the teal fabric and cut out using scissors. Iron or glue it onto the pocket. If gluing, avoid adhering the front of the pocket to the back by placing waxed paper or aluminum foil inside the pocket.

From Your Craft Cupboard

Fusible webbing or washable fabric glue (for fabrics)

Jewel glue or needle and thread (for buttons)

Tracing paper

Pencil

Straight pins

Ruler

Scissors and pinking shears

Iron and pressing cloth or light towel (if using fusible webbing)

Aluminum foil or waxed paper (if gluing)

3. Place tracing paper above the pants pockets, and trace the area from the waist to the side seam and down the curved opening of each of the two pockets (roughly a triangle with one curved side). Remove the tracing from the pants, and add about $\frac{1}{2}$" to the curve of the pocket opening. Pin the tracing to a solid fabric and cut out with scissors. Iron or glue onto the pocket opening, making sure the bottom of the fabric goes into the pocket to allow your hand to slide easily into the pocket.

4. Using the pinking shears, cut about seven $1\frac{1}{2}$" squares of the various color fabrics.

5. Iron or glue these fabric shapes to the overalls, scattering them at odd angles over the pants and placing one over the solid fabric covering the top pocket. Refer to the photo as a guide.

6. Cut $1\frac{1}{2}$" long pieces of rickrack. Glue 1 strip of rickrack on each of the fabric squares, near one edge.

7. Glue or stitch 1 button in the center of each fabric square. Choose a button color that contrasts with the color of the fabric.

Handkerchief Dress and Matching Shoes

Primary Technique: Sewing or Gluing

Start With...

Infant-size white T-shirt

White satin baby shoes

And Add...

Handkerchief with 3 corners and edges embroidered: 1 large and 2 small designs (or 3 separate handkerchiefs with matching designs)

Fabric: about 3" x 45" for skirt ruffle

Eyelet trim: ¾" x 45"

Then Simply...

For the Dress:

1. Lay the T-shirt flat on your work surface. Place tracing paper over the shirt and use a pencil to trace the neckline shape and about 2" across each shoulder.

2. Lay the handkerchief right side up; place the neckline tracing over it, across the corner with the large design. The ends of the shoulder seam lines should be at the embroidered edge. Pin in place and cut the handkerchief along the neckline of the tracing.

3. Stitch or use fabric glue to adhere the handkerchief to the front of the shirt, matching the neckline and shoulder seams

From Your Craft Cupboard

Tracing paper

Pencil   Scissors

Washable fabric glue (to attach handkerchief to shirt and shoes) **or needle and**

thread for hand stitching

Sewing machine (to add ruffle for skirt)

Aluminum foil or waxed paper (if gluing)

Tiny Tots' Tees

Counterclockwise from bottom left:

Handkerchief Dress and Shoes, Patchwork Puppy Shirt, Dapper Little Weskit, Tea Towel Romper

with the cut edge of the handkerchief and tucking it under the shoulder flaps of the shirt (see Diagram 3-1). If gluing, avoid adhering the front of the shirt to the back by placing waxed paper or aluminum foil between the layers.

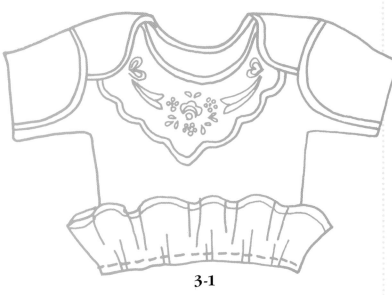

3-1

4. To add a ruffle at the bottom of the shirt, cut a 3" x 45" strip of fabric. Machine-overcast or hem one 45" side of the strip. Lay the eyelet trim right side up over the right side of the fabric along the other 45" side. Add a running stitch, by machine or hand, about ¼" down through the eyelet trim and the fabric; pull the thread to gather the fabric and eyelet to the length of the bottom of the shirt with the shirt bottom stretched as much as possible. Put the 3" ends of the strip together, with right side of the fabric and eyelet trim to the inside, and sew a ¼" seam. Align the gathered edge of the ruffle with the bottom of the shirt, right sides together. Pin, starting in the

center of the back with the seam in the ruffle, stretching the shirt bottom as you go. Stitch the ruffle onto the shirt, making a ¼" seam (see Diagram 3-1) .

For the Shoes:

1. Place the shoes on your work surface. Lay tracing paper over the front of each shoe and use a pencil to trace the shape across the top.

2. Lay the handkerchief right side up; place 1 shoe tracing over it, across 1 corner with a small design. The ends of the tracing lines should be at the embroidered edge. Pin in place and cut the handkerchief along the tracing line. Repeat for the other shoe.

3. Use fabric glue or hand stitch to attach the handkerchief to each shoe, matching the top edge with the cut edge of the handkerchief. If gluing the handkerchief to a shoe with a tongue and strap, as in the photo, avoid adhering the tongue to the strap by pinning the strap back out of the gluing area.

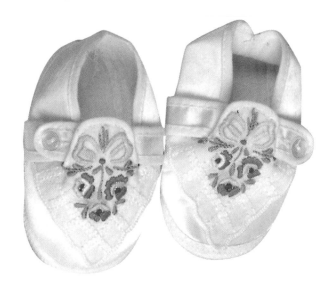

Patchwork Puppy Shirt

Primary Technique: Embroidery

Start With...

Baby shirt

And Add...

Fabric: 4" x 4" piece of antique patchwork or new patchwork print fabric

Button: ⅛", black

Embroidery floss: blue or other color to coordinate with patchwork

Tea bag

Puppy pattern on this page

From Your Craft Cupboard

Tracing paper and pencil

Straight pins

Scissors

Embroidery needle

Then Simply...

1. Tea-stain the baby shirt to give it an antique look. Fill a bowl with hot water and drop in the tea bag (remove the tag, if it has one). Submerge the shirt in the tea and soak it until it is the shade you like. Let dry.

2. Following the embroidery instructions on page 11, blanket-stitch around the armhole, neckline, and shoulder seams with blue floss.

3. Trace the puppy pattern on this page. Pin the tracing to the patchwork fabric and cut it out. Pin in place on the shirt, using the photo as a guide.

4. Blanket-stitch around the puppy to attach it to the shirt. Remove the pins.

5. Securely stitch on the black button for the puppy's eye.

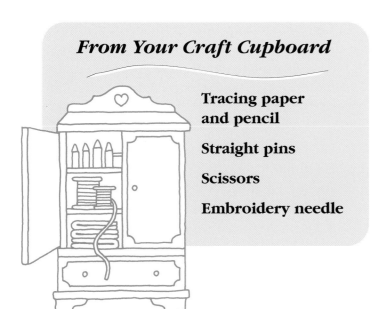

Dapper Little Weskit

Primary Technique: Gluing or Hand Stitching

Start With...

Baby shirt

And Add...

Handkerchief or tea towel: with an embroidered or appliquéd design repeated in 2 corners, about 8" square

Small button: $1/4$" – $3/8$"

From Your Craft Cupboard

Tracing paper

Pencil   **Ruler**

Scissors

Straight pins

Washable fabric glue or needle and thread (to attach handkerchief to shirt)

Aluminum foil or waxed paper (if gluing)

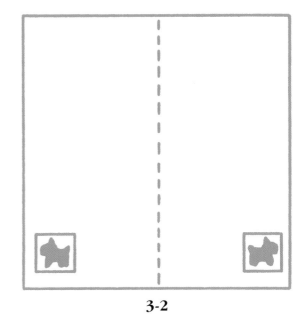

3-2

Then Simply...

1. Cut the handkerchief up the center front between the center designs (see Diagram 3-2). Cut tracing paper to the size of your handkerchief halves, and mark the position of the design on each.

2. Lay the shirt flat on your work surface. Lay the tracing paper over the shirt with the design at the bottom where you want the bottom of the vest to be (see Diagram 3-3). Angle the halves of the tracing paper slightly, spreading the corners below the design about $1/4$" apart (see Diagram 3-4 and refer to the photo). Remove 1 piece of the tracing paper and discard it.

76

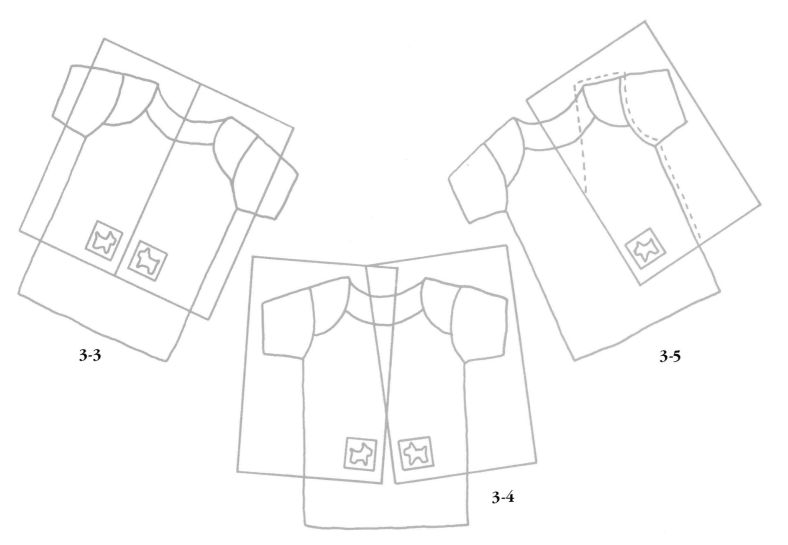

3-3

3-4

3-5

3. Trace the edges of the T-shirt onto the remaining piece of tracing paper, adding about ¼" outside the side seam, sleeve seam, and shoulder seam; stop drawing ¼" inside the neck opening. Use a ruler to draw a line from the neck opening on an angle to the center front of the shirt (see Diagram 3-5).

4. Lay the 2 halves of the handkerchief together with the right sides in and the designs overlapping. Lay the tracing over the handkerchief pieces, matching the design on the paper with the handkerchief designs. Pin in place and cut on the tracing lines.

5. Fold back ¼" on all the raw edges of the handkerchief and stitch or glue in place.

6. Lay the handkerchief pieces on the shirt in position and stitch or glue them down at the side seams, armholes, and shoulder seam. If gluing the handkerchief onto the shirt, place waxed paper or aluminum foil between the layers of the shirt to avoid gluing the front to the back.

7. Stitch on the button where the two handkerchief pieces overlap in the center of the shirt.

Tea Towel Romper

Primary Technique: Fusing or Gluing

Start With...

Pink romper (source: Sunbelt Sportswear)

And Add...

Antique tea towel: with one end embroidered with appropriate designs

Rickrack: baby size, 1 yard, pink

From Your Craft Cupboard

Tracing paper

Pencil   Scissors

Straight pins

Washable fabric glue or needle and thread (to attach trim and tea towel to romper)

Aluminum foil or waxed paper

Then Simply...

1. Lay the romper flat on your work surface. Place the tracing paper over the romper and use a pencil to trace the neckline, across the shoulder seams, the sleeve seam, and down the side seams to the length you want for the pinafore top (see Diagram 3-6).

2. Lay the tea towel right side up. Place the tracing over the towel with the embroidered area centered at the bottom (see Diagram 3-7). Pin in place and cut ¼" larger than the traced lines around the neck, shoulder, and armholes. If the tea towel is about the right width, you won't have to hem the sides.

3. Run a line of fabric glue around all raw edges and fold them back ¼" to form a finished edge (or hem by hand or sewing machine).

4. If gluing the towel onto the romper, place waxed paper or aluminum foil between the layers of the romper to avoid gluing the front to the back.

5. Turn the towel piece design side down on your work surface, and run a line of fabric glue on all the edges of the fabric that you have seamed—do not run glue along the bottom (prefinished hem). Smooth the glue

out to the edge of the fabric with your finger. Turn the towel over onto the romper, matching the neckline and other openings, and press in place with your hands. Let dry flat. As an alternative to gluing, you can hand-stitch the towel in place on the romper; do not stitch along the bottom (prefinished hem) of the towel.

6. Glue rickrack along the armholes, neckline, and bottom (finished) edge, using the photo as a guide.

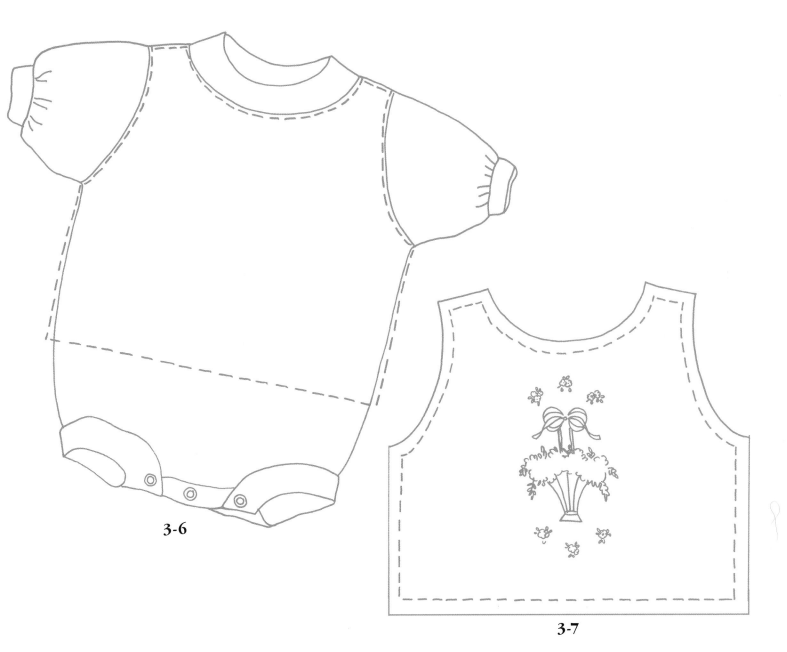

3-6

3-7

Cookie Cutter Pajamas

Primary Technique: Fusing or Gluing

Start With...

Red or white one-piece baby pajamas
(we used footed pajamas with a back flap;
source: The Active Edge)

And Add...

Plaid fabric: 4" x 12", red and green

Satin woven-edge ribbon: 1/8" x 6", red

Buttons: 2, 1/8"–3/16", white

Stars: 24, about 3/16", gold

Cookie cutters: 4, about 2"–4" across (to use as
patterns): bear, heart, moon, tree, or other suitable holiday designs, or use patterns on page 82

Dimensional fabric paint: with fine-line
applicator tip, dark green

Then Simply...

1. If using fusible webbing, iron it to the
back of the plaid fabric. Trace the 4 cookie
cutter shapes onto the front of the plaid
fabric with a white pencil or chalk. If
you prefer, use tracing paper and a pencil
to transfer the patterns on page 82. Pin
the tracing paper to the plaid fabric. Cut
out the 4 shapes.

From Your Craft Cupboard

White pencil or chalk

Tracing paper (if using
patterns)

Pencil (if using patterns)

Scissors

**Fusible webbing or
washable fabric glue**
(to attach cutouts)

**Needle and thread or
washable fabric glue** (for
attaching buttons and bows)

**Iron and pressing cloth
or light towel** (if using
fusible webbing)

**Aluminum foil or waxed
paper** (if gluing)

Bottoms Up

Cookie Cutter Pajamas

Cookie Cutter Pajamas appliqué patterns

2. Lay the fabric shapes on the front of the pajamas, as shown in photo. Attach using fusible webbing or fabric glue, following the fusing or gluing instructions on page 9. If gluing, avoid adhering the front of the pajamas to the back by placing waxed paper or aluminum foil between the layers.

3. Cut the 6" length of ribbon into two 3" pieces. Tie 2 small bows. Glue or stitch the bows to the neckline of the bear and the top of the heart.

4. Stitch the buttons to the front of the bear.

5. Glue 3 gold stars on the pajamas near the moon.

6. Glue the remaining stars on the Christmas tree, scattering them over the entire tree.

7. Run a fine line of dimensional fabric paint around each of the fabric shapes, making sure the paint touches both the pajamas and the edges of the fabric shapes to prevent fraying and loose edges.

8. Allow to dry.

Littlest Leaguer's Uniform

Primary Technique: Fusing or Gluing

Start With...

Baby's baseball-striped bubble suit
(source: The Active Edge)

And Add...

Flannel fabrics: 5" x 7" of plaid, 5" x 7" of check, 12" x 7" of black

Dimensional fabric paint: with fine-line applicator tip, black

Number patterns on page 85

From Your Craft Cupboard

Tracing paper

Pencil

Straight pins

Scissors

Fusible webbing or washable fabric glue (to attach fabric cutouts)

Iron and pressing cloth or light towel (if using fusible webbing)

Aluminum foil or waxed paper (if gluing)

Then Simply...

1. If using fusible webbing, iron it on the back of all the fabrics, following the fusing instructions on page 9. Turn the fabrics right side up.

2. Use tracing paper and a pencil to trace the number patterns on the facing page. Be sure to trace both the outer and inner lines. Pin the tracings on the front side of the black fabric and cut out the numbers on the outer lines. Remove the tracings from the black fabric; use those same tracings to cut out 1 number from the checked fabric and 1 from the plaid fabric, cutting on the inner lines of the tracings.

3. Lay the black fabric numbers on the front of the baby suit, using the photo as a guide. Fuse or glue in place. If gluing, avoid adhering the front of the suit to the back by placing waxed paper or aluminum foil between the layers.

4. Center the plaid and checked numbers in place over the black fabric numbers. Fuse or glue in place.

5. Run a thin line of dimensional fabric paint around the black numbers where they meet the suit and around the plaid and checked numbers where they meet the black numbers. Be sure the paint touches both the suit and the edge of the fabric. This prevents fraying and loose edges.

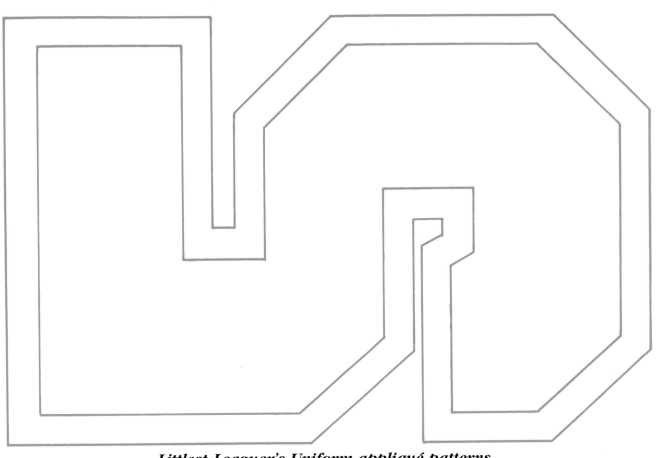

Littlest Leaguer's Uniform appliqué patterns

Wee Ones' Tux and Formal

Primary Techniques: Gluing (on boy's shirt) and Sewing (on girl's dress)

Start With...

Baby-size T-shirt

And Add...

To the Boy's Shirt:

Polka-dot ribbon: black and white, 1½" x 8"

Bias tape: 72" of black, 36" of white

Buttons: 5 or 6, ⅛", black

Cummerbund pattern on page 88

To the Girl's Shirt:

Polka-dot fabric: 6" x 45"

Ribbon roses with leaves: 1 small, 1 large, red

Satin picot-edged ribbon: 3/16" x 12", red

Heart appliqué: small, white

Then Simply...

For the Boy's Shirt:

1. Cut 9 pieces of black bias tape, each 8" long, to make the cummerbund. Place 1 piece lengthwise on your work surface, and run a thin line of glue near the bottom edge. Place the edge of another piece over the glue line, and smooth down. Run a thin line of glue at the bottom of that piece; place another piece over the glue line, and smooth down.

From Your Craft Cupboard

Tracing paper Pencil	**Sewing machine and notions** (for girl's dress)
Straight pins Scissors	
Washable fabric glue	**Aluminum foil or waxed paper** (if gluing)
Needle and thread for hand stitching	

Steppin' Out
Wee Ones' Tux *(left)* and Formal *(right)*

Repeat until all 9 black bias tape pieces have been used. This should form a rectangle about 3" x 8". Lay aside to dry.

2. Cut 6 pieces of white bias tape, each 6" long, to make the pleats for the front of the shirt. Glue groups of 3 together, as you did in Step 1.

3. Lay the 2 groups of pleats vertically on the center front of the shirt with about ¾" between them. Trim to fit the shape of the shoulder seam at the top. Run a thin line of glue around all the edges of the pleat rectangles, and smooth in place on the front of the shirt. Avoid adhering the front of the shirt to the back by placing aluminum foil or waxed paper between the layers of the shirt.

4. Use the tracing paper and a pencil to trace the pattern for the cummerbund, below. Pin the tracing paper on the front of the black bias tape rectangle, and cut out the cummerbund.

5. Run a thin line of fabric glue around the outside edges of the cummerbund on the back of the bias tape. Place the straight line of the cummerbund at the bottom of the shirt, with the curved part at the top, and smooth into place. The cummerbund will overlap the bottom of the shirt pleats.

6. Run a thin line of fabric glue around the cut edges of the cummerbund and on the top edge of the pleats where they meet the shirt. Be sure the glue touches both the shirt and the edge of the bias tape to prevent fraying.

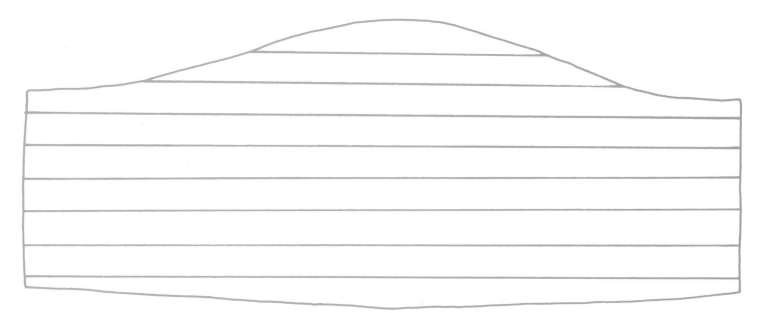

Wee Ones' Tux cummerbund pattern

7. Use the polka-dot ribbon to form a bow, bringing both ends to the middle, pinching together, and stitching in place. Stitch to the shirt at the center neckline.

8. Measure every ¾" down the center front of the shirt below the tie, and securely sew on the buttons.

For the Girl's Dress:

1. Cut the polka-dot fabric into 2 strips: one 2½" wide and one 3½" wide. Tightly zigzag or serge one 45" edge of each strip to finish the edge.

2. Lay the 2½" strip on top of the 3½" strip, both right side up, with the raw edges together; pin in place. Bring the ends of the strips together, right sides together, and straight-stitch a ¼" seam along the 3½" end. Turn right side out.

3. Run a gathering stitch near the raw edge of the strips. Pull the thread to gather until the ruffle is the same width as the bottom of the T-shirt. Put the gathered edge of the ruffle, right side out, about ½" under the hemline of the shirt; the right side of the ruffle should face the wrong side of the shirt. Pin the ruffle and the shirt together with the ruffle seam at the center back. Baste the ruffle to the shirt with a long running stitch; remove the pins. With the shirt right side out, topstitch through the ruffle and shirt at the bottom fold of the shirt hem.

4. Glue or stitch the heart appliqué to the center front of the dress. Glue or stitch a small rose to the center of the heart.

5. Tie the red ribbon into a bow with tails, and glue or stitch it to the right front of the dress where the ruffle begins. Glue or stitch a large rose to the center of the ribbon.

Pinafore from the Linen Closet

Primary Technique: Sewing

Start With...

Linen guest towel: 1, about 12" x 18", with crocheted edging and openwork design, white

Pillowcases: 2, standard-size, white

And Add...

White fabric: 8" square (for facing)

Seam binding: white

Grosgrain ribbon: 3/16" x 32", white

From Your Craft Cupboard

Fabric marker with disappearing ink

Ruler or yardstick

Scissors

Sewing machine and notions

Needle and white thread for hand stitching

Iron

Then Simply...

1. To make the pinafore top, refer to Diagram 3-8 for neckline and back opening measurements, and mark them with your fabric marker on the guest towel. The outside measurements of the towel are 18" long by 12" wide. A 4" square hole is cut for the neck 7½" up from the bottom at the center of the towel, and the back opening is cut from the plain edge up to the neck. (*Note:* Adjust size for a smaller or larger child by reducing or increasing these measurements, as needed; measure your child or a dress in the correct size.)

2. To form the facing for the neck opening, use the 8" square of white fabric. Referring to Diagram 3-9, draw a 4" opening in the center of the square (2" of fabric all around it). In the center of one side, cut a slit for the back opening.

3. Put the right side of the pinafore and the right side of the facing together, with the back opening slits together. Stitch around the 4" square neck opening, making a ¼" seam. Clip from each corner to within ¹⁄₁₆" of the seam at each of the corners (see Diagram 3-10).

4. Turn right side out and bind the raw edges of the facing.

Christmas Angel
Pinafore from the Linen Closet

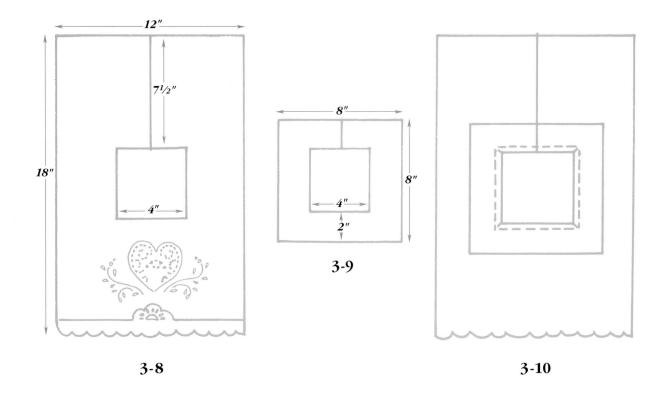

3-8

3-9

3-10

5. Stitch on the top side of the fabric around the neckline about ¼" from the neck opening to be sure the facing will lie flat on the inside of the pinafore.

6. Bring the bottom edges of the front and the back together at the sides, right sides facing; stitch together at each side, from the bottom up, about 1". This defines the armhole. Spread the seams open and iron them back.

7. To make the pinafore skirt, take 1 pillowcase and open the side and end seams to form the front of the skirt. Then open the side and end seams of the other pillowcase and cut on the folded side to make 2 pillowcase halves for the back of the skirt. Sew one pillowcase half to each side of

the skirt front, right sides together, with a ¼" seam. Fold the raw edges ¼" to the back and iron in place. Fold back another ¼" and stitch to make a finished hem. These hemmed edges will be the opening in the center back of the pinafore skirt.

8. Adjust the skirt length for your child. Most standard-size pillowcases are about 28" long; you may use that entire length, if you wish, or cut off any excess length across the raw edge of the pillowcase. Our skirt is about 20" long.

9. Run a gathering stitch along the top (the raw edge), about ¼" from the edge. Pull the gathering stitch evenly to make the gathered skirt the same width as the bottom of the pinafore top (about 24").

10. Lay the pillowcase skirt flat on your work surface with the right side up. Align the bottom edge of the guest towel with the gathered edge of the skirt, with the right sides together and the back openings matching. Pin the towel to the pillowcase skirt, pushing the towel's crocheted edging down between the two as you go; the crocheted edging should not be between the skirt and the top when you pin them together. Baste together, being careful not to catch the crochet in the stitching; remove the pins. If you prefer, fold the crocheted edging up on the right side of the towel and pin it out of the way before you join the top to the skirt.

11. Turn the pinafore right side out. Smooth the crocheted edging down over the skirt in the front and check the basted seam in the back. Then topstitch all around the top as shown in Diagram 3-11.

12. Cut four 8" lengths of grosgrain ribbon to be tie closures for the pinafore. Stitch them to the hemmed edges of the right and left sides of the back opening at the neck and the waist.

3-11

A Touch of Romance

Lovely laces, delicate doilies,
and pretty pearls adorn these fashions
inspired by the Victorian era.
Even a basic black jacket takes on
the elegance of a bygone
age with the addition of such
luxurious touches.

Ballerina Shirt and Matching Hat

Primary Technique: Fusing or Gluing

Start With...

Ivory, long-sleeve ballerina shirt (source: Sunbelt)

Ivory hat with floppy brim: felt or velour

And Add...

To the Shirt:

Moiré fabric: 5" x 15", tan

Muted floral print fabric: about 3" x 10"

Lace and/or crocheted pieces: assorted straight and curved lengths, approximately 2" x 24", ecru or ivory

Pearl string: about 36" long, 4 mm, ivory

Charms: 4, about 1"–1½", hearts, mirror, bow, hand, etc., goldtone

Buttons: 4, various sizes ½"–¾", in colors to coordinate with floral fabric

Ribbon roses with leaves: 2, small, in a color to coordinate with floral fabric

Dimensional fabric paint: with fine-line applicator tip, pearlescent white

To the Hat:

Lace: about 1½" x 24" (measure width and length of your hat brim for exact measurements), ecru

Charm: 1, 1"–1½", goldtone

Ribbon rose with leaves: 1, small, coordinated with colors on shirt

From Your Craft Cupboard

Fusible webbing or washable fabric glue (for fabrics)

Freezer paper (if using fusible webbing)

Jewel glue (for pearls, charms, and buttons)

Washable fabric glue (for hat lace and ribbon roses)

Ruler   Scissors

Iron and pressing cloth or light towel (if using fusible webbing)

T-shirt board or aluminum foil or waxed paper (if gluing)

Then Simply...

For the Shirt:

1. If using fusible webbing, iron it on the back of the all the fabrics, following the fusing instructions on page 9. Put freezer paper over lace before ironing.

2. Cut 3 squares of moiré fabric, each 5" x 5".

3. Using the photo and Diagrams 4-1, 4-2, and 4-3 as guides, cut pieces of floral fabric to overlap the moiré on 2 of the squares.

4. Cut lace or crocheted pieces as shown in the photo and the diagrams.

5. Fuse or glue the floral fabric and the lace/crochet pieces to the moiré. If fusing, place freezer paper between iron and lace. If gluing, avoid adhering the front of the shirt to the back by using a T-shirt board or placing waxed paper or aluminum foil between the layers.

6. Using the photo as a guide, place the 3 moiré squares on the shirt front at odd angles. Attach using fusible webbing or fabric glue, as before.

7. Glue on pearl strands, charms, small ribbon roses, and buttons, as shown in the diagrams. For pearls, run a fine line of jewel glue on the fabric where the pearls will be placed, then press the pearl strand into the glue; trim off excess at end.

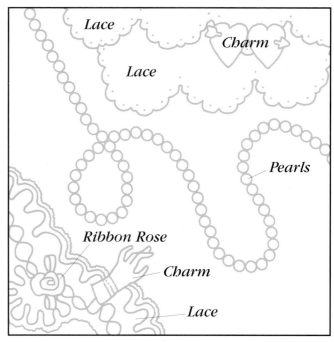

4-1

Apply glue to the back of the charms, roses, and buttons, then press them into place on the fabric.

8. Run a fine line of dimensional fabric paint around the outside edge of the moiré squares, making sure the paint touches both the fabric edge and the shirt. This prevents fraying and loose edges. Allow to dry flat for 24 hours.

For the Hat:

1. Fold the brim back to the crown of the hat at the front and glue or stitch it in place at that spot only.

2. Choose a lace the width of the hat brim or slightly narrower; cut the length to allow

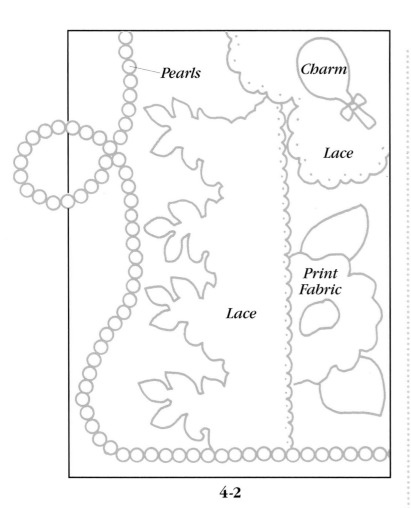

4-2

the lace to go completely around the underside of the brim. Spread a thin layer of fabric glue on the back of the lace with your finger. Start at the back of the hat, under the brim, and press the lace to the brim; continue completely around the hat brim.

3. Glue a small ribbon rose and a charm over the lace at the front of the hat, as shown in the photo. Allow to dry.

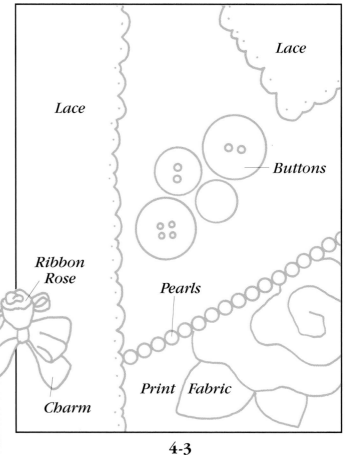

4-3

Lacy Crocheted Jacket

Primary Technique: Hand Sewing

Start With...

2 white crocheted table runners with repeated circle pattern (source: Peking Handicrafts)

And Add...

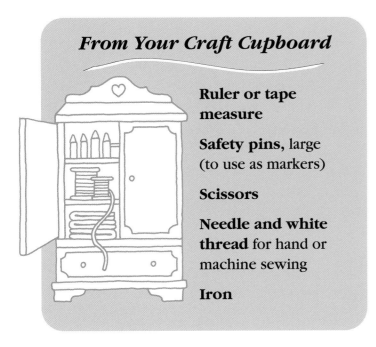

From Your Craft Cupboard

Ruler or tape measure

Safety pins, large (to use as markers)

Scissors

Needle and white thread for hand or machine sewing

Iron

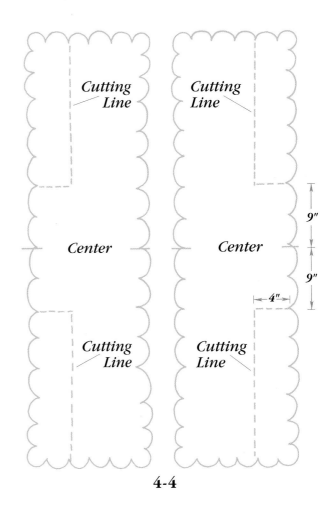

4-4

Then Simply...

1. Fold one of the table runners in half across the short width. Put a safety pin in to mark the center of the runner. Repeat with the other runner.

2. Open the table runners and lay them flat on your work surface right side up. Mark for cutting as indicated on Diagram 4-4; since you will be cutting between the circles, not through them, always mark at the edge of the nearest whole circle. Start at the center pin, measure down one side of the runner about 9", and pin to mark at the nearest whole circle. Start at the center pin, measure in the opposite direction about 9", and pin to mark at the nearest whole circle.

3. Measure 4" across the runner from the markers you placed in Step 2, and pin to mark at the nearest whole circle.

4. Use a ruler or tape measure to find the points at the ends of the runner that are straight up and down from the places you marked in Step 3. Mark them with pins. Be sure you have marked at the nearest whole circle.

5. Cut out the rectangle formed by the pins you placed in Steps 2, 3, and 4. Remember to cut between the circles. (Save leftover pieces of crocheted runner to use as embellishments for other projects.)

6. Repeat for the other runner, except that you will be cutting from the other side, to form the left and right sides of the jacket.

7. Put the right sides of the runners together and make a ½" seam (see Diagram 4-5) either by hand or by machine. To allow neckline space, stitch from the bottom to within about 3" from the center of the runners.

8. Fold the runners in half to form the jacket shape as in Diagram 4-6, and stitch ½" side and underarm seams. Spread the seams open and iron them flat.

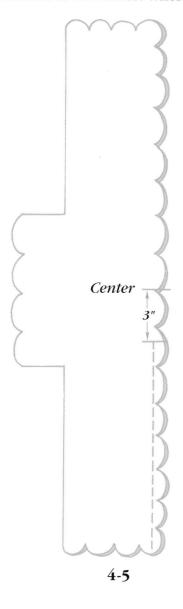

Center

3"

4-5

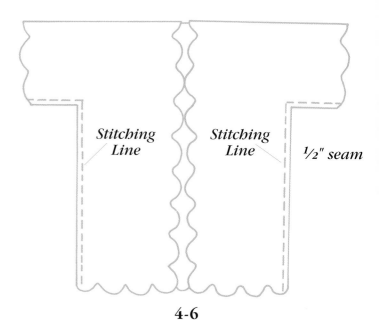

Stitching Line

Stitching Line

½" seam

4-6

Tees for Two

Left: **Doily Cutaway Shirt**
Right: **Nosegay and Ribbon Vee**

Doily Cutaway Shirt

Primary Technique: Sewing or Gluing

Start With...

T-shirt without pocket

And Add...

Crocheted doilies: 5, round or heart-shaped, white or ecru

Ribbon roses with leaves: 7, small, colors to coordinate with shirt (we used 2 lavender and 5 pink)

From Your Craft Cupboard

Scissors: small, sharp-pointed

Washable fabric glue or sewing machine (to attach doilies)

T-shirt board or aluminum foil or waxed paper (if gluing)

Then Simply...

1. Cut the ribbing off the neckline of the shirt. Fold under and make a narrow hem by hand or machine.

2. Place 3 doilies across the front of the shirt, between the bustline and the shoulder seam, with 1 centered and 1 on each side of the front. Place another doily on each sleeve (use photo as a guide).

3. Sew the doilies in place, topstitching them around the outer edge, or use fabric glue to attach them to the shirt. If gluing, avoid adhering the front of the shirt to the back by using a T-shirt board or placing waxed paper or aluminum foil between the layers. Allow to dry.

4. Turn the shirt inside out. Cut out the fabric of the shirt behind each doily up to the stitch or glue line, being very careful not to cut through the doily.

5. Sew or glue ribbon roses in the centers of the doilies: 3 on the middle doily and 1 on each of the other 4 doilies.

Nosegay and Ribbon Vee

Primary Techniques: Fusing and Gluing

Start With...

V-neck T-shirt (ours is size L, adjust materials for larger or smaller sizes)

And Add...

V-shaped lace appliqué: 2" wide, about 14" long (measure from shoulder to point of neck; may need 2 to extend length), with floral design (if available), white

Loose pearls: about 150, 4 mm, white

Pearl string: 28" long, 4 mm, white

Picot-edge ribbon: ³/₁₆" x 28", peach

Ribbon roses with leaves: 5, large, peach

Then Simply...

1. Place the shirt on a T-shirt board or lay it on a flat work surface.

2. Lay the appliqué just beneath the seam of the T-shirt neckline, placing the V of the appliqué at the V of the shirt neck. If the appliqué is not long enough to reach the shoulder seams, use a second appliqué to extend the length, cutting and using only the straight sides.

3. Use fusible webbing or fabric glue to attach the lace appliqué to the shirt, following the fusing or gluing instructions on page 9. If fusing, place freezer paper between lace

---

From Your Craft Cupboard

Fusible webbing or washable fabric glue (to attach appliqué)

Freezer paper (if using fusible webbing)

Washable fabric glue (to attach ribbon and ribbon roses)

Jewel glue (for pearls and pearl strings)

Ruler   Scissors

Iron and pressing cloth or light towel (if using fusible webbing)

T-shirt board or aluminum foil or waxed paper

and iron. If gluing, avoid adhering the front of the shirt to the back by using a T-shirt board or placing waxed paper or aluminum foil between the layers.

4. Glue on pearls at the ends of the petals in the floral motifs of the appliqué or scattered about every ½" over the whole appliqué, as shown in the photo. Put a dot of jewel glue on the appliqué where each pearl will be placed, then press the pearl into the glue.

5. Cut the pearl strand and the ribbon in half. Glue 1 piece of the ribbon and pearl strand at the center of the V of the appliqué; give a twist to the ribbon and pearl strand and glue it to the appliqué; repeat twisting and gluing about every 2". When you are about 2" from the shoulder seam, form a loop of the ribbon and pearl string about 2" long and glue the ends to the last spot you had glued the ribbon and pearl string. Repeat for the other side of the appliqué.

6. Glue 1 ribbon rose near each shoulder where you glued the ends of the ribbon and pearl strand. Glue the remaining 3 roses at the center of the V of the appliqué, where you started gluing the ends of the ribbon and pearl strands.

Striking Contrasts

Left: **Lace-Edged Sweater**
Right: **Handkerchief-Trimmed Jacket
and Body Suit**

Lace-Edged Sweater

Primary Technique: Gluing

Start With...

Black short-sleeve sweater

And Add...

Heavyweight lace: 2" x 72", white

V-shaped lace appliqué: about 5" wide and 3" high, white

Pearl string: 8", 3 mm, white

Wire-edged ribbon: ¾" x 8", pastel color

Charm: 1, about 1 ¼", cherub or other design, goldtone

From Your Craft Cupboard

Washable fabric glue (for lace and appliqué)

Jewel glue (for pearls, charm, and ribbon bow)

Scissors

T-shirt board or aluminum foil or waxed paper

Then Simply...

1. Following the gluing instructions on page 9, glue the lace around the sleeves and the bottom of the sweater. Always start and end at the seam, and cut the lace cleanly to make joined ends attractive. Avoid adhering the front of the sweater to the back by using a T-shirt board or placing waxed paper or aluminum foil between the layers.

2. Glue the appliqué to the front of the sweater just below the collar ribbing.

3. Fold the two ends of the wired ribbon in to the center, and pinch the center of the ribbon together, through all layers, to form a bow.

4. Cut two 3" lengths of pearl string. Use jewel glue to attach one end of each of the 2 strands to the center point of the appliqué; let the bottom ends hang free. Glue the bow on top of the glued ends of the pearl strands. Glue the cherub to the center of the bow.

Handkerchief-Trimmed Jacket and Body Suit

Primary Techniques: Fusing, Gluing and Sewing

Start With...

Dark suit jacket or blazer (we used a man's)

White V-neckline body suit

And Add...

To the Jacket:

Handkerchiefs with cutwork edges and 1 large corner motif: 4, approximately 12" square, white (source: Peking Handicrafts)

To the Body Suit:

Handkerchief with cutwork edges and 1 large corner motif: 1, approximately 12" square, white (source: Peking Handicrafts)

Ribbon rose with leaves: 1, large, color of your choice

Then Simply...

For the Jacket:

1. Press the 4 handkerchiefs flat with the iron. Lay the jacket on your work surface face up. You will be marking, cutting, fusing, and stitching the handkerchiefs onto the jacket to decorate the collar and lapels (2 handkerchiefs) and the sleeve cuffs (2 handkerchiefs).

From Your Craft Cupboard

Fusible webbing	Scissors
Washable fabric glue	Iron and pressing cloth or light towel
Pencil or fabric marker with disappearing ink	Freezer paper

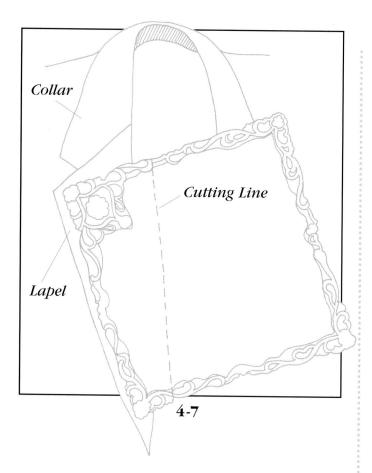

Collar

Cutting Line

Lapel

4-7

3. Repeat Step 2 using another handkerchief on the opposite lapel, but turn the handkerchief to have the corner motif in the correct position. Lay those pieces aside.

4. Use the leftover pieces from the two handkerchiefs you cut in Steps 2 and 3 to cover the collar, as shown in Diagram 4-8. Put the corner of one piece of handkerchief at the upper collar point; wrap the edge of the handkerchief around the collar following the outer edge to the center back. Cut off the excess handkerchief as you did in Step 2, leaving about 1" to wrap around to the inside when you attach the handkerchief to the jacket. Cut the excess length of handkerchief off at the center back, leaving about ¼" extra on each side; fold

2. Take 1 handkerchief and lay it on one of the lapels of the jacket, with the large corner motif at the point, as shown in Diagram 4-7. The edge of the handkerchief will follow the outer edge of the lapel as it extends down the jacket; the edge at the top of the motif will follow the seam between the collar and lapel. Use your pencil to draw a line on the handkerchief about 1" wider than the lapel; this excess will wrap around to the inside when you attach the handkerchief to the jacket.Cut the handkerchief on the line. Fold under ¼" of the raw edge and glue to make a "hemmed" edge.

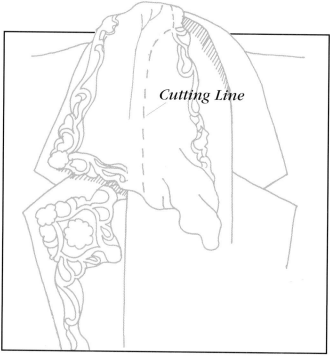

Cutting Line

4-8

4-9

back all raw edges ¼" and glue to make a "hemmed" edge. Repeat for the other collar, remembering to turn that handkerchief piece so the corner is in the correct position on the collar.

5. Use fusible webbing, following the fusing instructions on page 9, to attach the four pieces of handkerchief to the lapels of the jacket. To preserve your iron, place freezer paper on top of cutwork before ironing. Wrap the excess width of the handkerchief around the lapel to the inside of the jacket. The two "hemmed" edges of the collar pieces should just meet at the center back, without overlapping. You may want to top-stitch the handkerchiefs to the lapels and collar, and hand-stitch the handkerchiefs to the fabric inside for a more finished look.

6. Cut the sleeves off the jacket at whatever length you like, then use the handkerchiefs to make cuffs. Fold a whole handkerchief in half, between two undecorated corners, forming a triangle with the large corner motif entirely visible; cut on the fold and repeat with another handkerchief (save the undecorated halves of the handkerchiefs in your scrap bag). Pin 1 decorated handkerchief triangle, center point up, at the bottom of each sleeve, as shown in Diagram 4-9, starting with the motif at the center outside of the sleeve and working around the sleeve toward the seam on the inside; as you did on the lapels, leave about 1" extra handkerchief material below the bottom of the sleeve to fold up to the inside. Fuse to the sleeve. If you stitched the handkerchiefs to the lapels in Step 5, do so on the sleeves.

For the Body Suit:

1. Cut only the large corner motif from a complete handkerchief.

2. Use fusible webbing to attach it to the center front of the body suit, just below the point of the neckline. Place freezer paper between handkerchief piece and iron.

3. Hand-sew or glue on a ribbon rose in the center of the motif.

Funky and Folky

Flowers, tie dye, denim, and beads—a return to the '60s? No, it's retro dressing with an emphasis on fun. The accessories, including matching headbands and floppy hats, are perfect finishing touches for the totally funky look. Here, too, the international flavors of bright fabrics and folk-inspired designs turn ordinary garments into exotic creations.

Sunshine and
Moonbeams

Left: **Multicolored
Embroidered Shirt**

Right: **Sunflower
Vest and Cap**

Multicolored Embroidered Shirt

Primary Technique: Embroidery

Start With...

Blue chambray shirt
(source: Sunbelt Sportswear)

And Add...

**Embroidery floss in a variety of colors
of your choice**

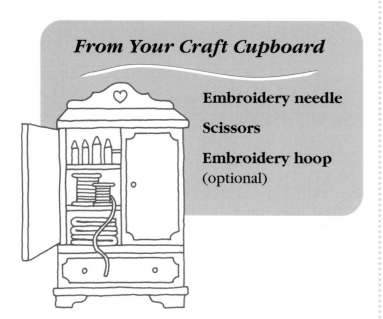

From Your Craft Cupboard

Embroidery needle

Scissors

Embroidery hoop
(optional)

Then Simply...

1. Review embroidery instructions on
pages 11-12. Choose a variety of stitches to
embroider along the natural guidelines of
the shirt, the seams.

2. Clean out your scrapbasket and use
up those odds and ends of floss; even
variegated floss is interesting.

3. Stitch around the pockets and down the
placket on the shirt front, changing floss
color for each area. And don't forget to do
some stitches on the back of the shirt, too!

4. This can be an ongoing project. Wear the
shirt and enjoy it, and when you don't have
it on, keep it handy and add a few stitches
here and there.

Sunflower Vest and Cap

Primary Techniques: Gluing and Embroidery

Start With...

Black felt, 24" x 48" (or a black vest)

Yellow baseball-style cap

And Add...

To the Felt Vest:

Felt: 5" x 5" green, 13" x 13" yellow

Plaid fabric: 5" x 5", black and cream

Buttons: 16, assorted brown

Dimensional fabric paint: with fine-line applicator tip, green and orange

Embroidery floss: red

Vest pattern on pages 62–63 (or a black vest)

Sunflower patterns on pages 114 and 115

To the Cap:

Buttons: 24–40, assorted brown

From Your Craft Cupboard

Tracing paper

Graphite paper: black

Pencil

Straight pins

White chalk

Ruler or yardstick

Scissors

Embroidery needle

Washable fabric glue (to attach fabric cutouts)

Jewel glue (for buttons on cap)

T-shirt board or aluminum foil or waxed paper

Then Simply...

For the Vest:

1. This vest is made exactly the same way as the Felt Appliquéd Vest shown on page 57. Follow the instructions in Steps 1–5 on pages 56–59.

2. Trace the patterns for the sunflowers and leaves, including the interior lines, on this page and page 115. Pin the traced patterns for the sunflowers on the yellow felt and cut out. Pin the leaf patterns on the green felt and cut out. Cut the 2 round centers of the sunflowers from the plaid fabric. Lay the tracings aside, but keep them.

Sunflower Vest appliqué patterns

3. Using the photo as a guide, position the felt shapes on the vest front, the larger flower on the left, as you face the vest, the smaller flower on the right. Use a thin layer of fabric glue to attach them. Avoid adhering the front of the vest to the back by using a T-shirt board or placing waxed paper or aluminum foil between the layers.

4. Lay graphite paper over one sunflower, colored side down. Lay the flower tracing over the graphite, looking underneath to be sure the pattern and the felt flower are matched. Trace over the interior lines of the flower. Repeat for the other sunflower and for the green leaves.

5. Run thin lines of dimensional fabric paint over the flower and leaf detail lines you just transferred and around all edges: orange on the sunflowers and green on the leaves. Allow to dry.

6. When the paint is dry, glue the plaid centers to the felt sunflowers. Run a thin line of orange dimensional fabric paint around the centers.

7. Thread all 6 strands of red floss into the embroidery needle. Stitch a button in the center of each flower and scattered above the flowers on the vest.

8. Review instructions for blanket stitch on pages 11–12. Embroider around edge and armholes of vest.

For the Cap:

1. Scatter assorted buttons on the bill of the cap. When the arrangement is pleasing, glue each of the buttons down with the jewel glue.

Tie-Dyed Tee and Matching Hat Rosette

Primary Technique: Dyeing

Start With...

White T-shirt

Black floppy-brimmed hat

And Add...

To the Shirt:

Dye Ties™**:** cords impregnated with dye, purple assortment #32120 (source: Distlefink)

Jewels: 20, heart- or star-shaped

To the Hat:

Strip of T-shirt fabric: 3" x 24"

Dye Ties™**:** as for the shirt

Then Simply...

For the Shirt:

1. Wash the shirt before dyeing to remove any sizing; do not use fabric softener. Take the shirt damp dry from the washing machine or dampen it when you are ready to dye it.

2. Accordion-fold the body and sleeves of the shirt, starting at the bottom and working to the top of the shirt. Wrap Dye Ties™ around the shirt as shown in Diagram 5-1, and tie securely.

3. Follow the manufacturer's instructions for dyeing either in your microwave oven or in a pot of boiling water. If you will be making the rosette for the hat, dye the 3" x 24" strip of fabric along with the shirt.

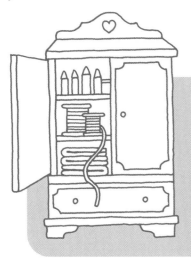

From Your Craft Cupboard

Rubber gloves

Scissors   Jewel glue

Needle and white thread

Washable fabric glue (optional)

T-shirt board or aluminum foil or waxed paper

Go with the Flow
Top: **Tie-Dyed Tee and Matching Hat Rosette;**
Bottom: **Reverse Tie-Dyed Jeans**

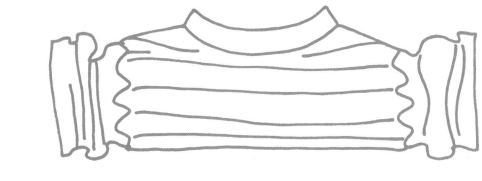

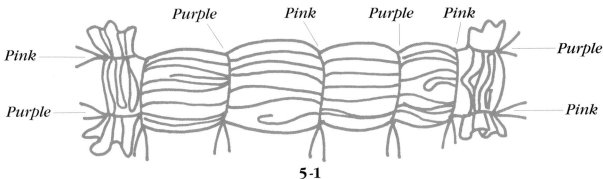

Pink — Purple — Pink — Purple — Pink — Purple — Pink

5-1

4. Using rubber gloves, carefully remove the shirt from the dye. Rinse the shirt under cold running water until it runs clear.

5. Cut the Dye Ties off, taking care not to cut the shirt. Smooth the shirt out flat to dry.

6. After the shirt is dry, glue on the jewels. Avoid adhering the front of the shirt to the back by using a T-shirt board or placing waxed paper or aluminum foil between the layers. Scatter the jewels over the shirt, using the design you've created with the dye as a guide to where to put the jewels. Allow to dry.

For the Hat:

1. Let the dyed strip of fabric dry.

2. Fold the strip in half lengthwise with the right side in, to form a 1½" x 24" rectangle. Stitch a ¼" seam along the open edge and down one 1½" end to the fold. Turn this strip right side out; push the open end into the tube about ¼" and whipstitch closed. Iron flat. Roll the strip of fabric into a rosette: Starting at one end of the fabric strip, grasping the seamed side in one hand and turning until the entire length of the fabric is rolled up around itself; hand-stitch together at the bottom (seamed side), making sure the stitches go through all layers of the fabric so the rosette doesn't come apart.

3. Fold back the brim of the hat to the crown near the front. Glue with fabric glue or hand-stitch in place.

4. Glue or stitch the rosette to the brim where you folded it back. Allow to dry.

Reverse Tie-Dyed Jeans

Primary Technique: Bleaching

Start With...

Dark blue jeans

And Add...

Bleach

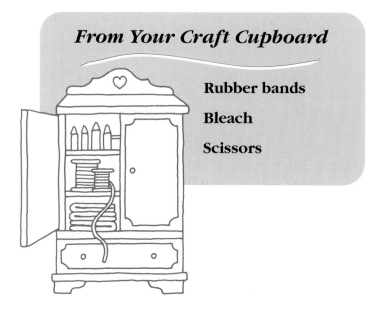

From Your Craft Cupboard

Rubber bands

Bleach

Scissors

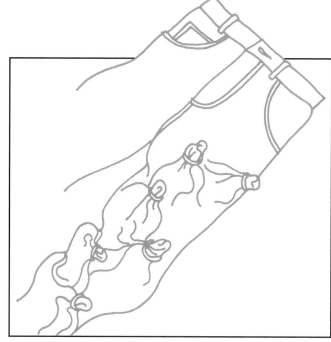

5-2

(see Diagram 5-2). Attach as many rubber bands as you wish; the more you use, the more blue areas there will be on the bleached jeans.

Then Simply...

1. Dampen the jeans.

2. Gather up the fabric of the jeans with your fingers, folding and crushing it as you go. Place rubber bands around the fabric

3. Fill a large sink with hot tap water. Add 2 cups of bleach. Submerge the jeans in the bleach. Leave in the sink for about 30 minutes. Turn over once to be sure all areas are soaked by the bleach water.

4. Remove the jeans from the bleach water and cut off the rubber bands carefully so you don't cut the fabric of the jeans.

5. Put the jeans in the washing machine on a cold wash cycle with no soap. Dry in dryer.

Sunflower Jeans with Matching Shirt and Hat

Primary Techniques: Sewing (on jeans);
Fusing or Gluing (on shirt and hat)

Start With...

Denim jeans

Navy ribbed-knit scoop-neck shirt

Black soft-brimmed hat

And Add...

To the Jeans:

Sunflower-print fabric: 1 yard, 45" wide

To the Shirt:

Sunflower-print fabric: ⅛ yard

Dimensional fabric paint: with fine-point
applicator tip, black or dark blue

To the Hat:

Silk sunflower

From Your Craft Cupboard

Fusible webbing
(about ¼ yard) **or
washable fabric glue**

**Yardstick or tape
measure**

Scissors

Straight pins

**Sewing machine and
notions**

Needle and thread for hand stitching
(optional)

Iron and pressing cloth or light towel
(if using fusible webbing)

**T-shirt board or aluminum foil or
waxed paper** (if gluing)

Woodstock Forever

Left: **Sunflower Jeans, Shirt, and Hat**
Center: **Crackled and Beaded Shirt and Headband**
Right: **Label-Pocket Tee**

Then Simply...

For the Jeans:

1. Try the jeans on and pin below each knee where you want the sunflower ruffle to be. Remove the jeans and lay them on a flat work surface. Cut off the bottom of the jeans on a horizontal line at the pins.

2. Measure the length of the fabric you cut off. Cut a strip of sunflower fabric 45" wide and the length of the jeans fabric you cut off plus 3".

3. Fold the sunflower fabric in half, right side in, with the two shorter ends together. Pin in place, and stitch a ¼" seam down that edge. Run a gathering stitch along one 45" edge of the loop; pull the thread until the length of the gathered edge matches the length along the bottom of the jeans. Pin the gathered edge of the print fabric to the bottom edge of the jeans, with the right sides of the fabric together (the jeans leg will be inside the print fabric). Stitch to attach with a ¼" seam. Repeat on the other leg. Turn print fabric down.

4. Hem the sunflower ruffle. Fold ¼" of the sunflower-print fabric toward the back of the fabric at the bottom edge, and run a straight stitch near the fold. Fold in a 2" hem, and pin in place. Try the jeans on to check the length; if the length of the sunflower fabric is too long or too short, adjust the size of the hem. Stitch the hem by hand or machine.

For the Shirt:

1. If you are using fusible webbing, apply it to the back of the sunflower fabric, following the fusing instructions on page 9.

2. Cut out about 20 sunflowers, including leaves.

3. Referring to the photo as a guide, place a ring of sunflowers about 2" below the neckline. Move the flowers, overlapping them, until you get a pleasant arrangement. Fuse or glue in place. If gluing, avoid adhering the front of the shirt to the back by using a T-shirt board or placing waxed paper or aluminum foil between the layers.

4. Run a thin line of dimensional fabric paint around all the flowers where they meet the shirt and where they overlap. Be sure the paint touches both the edge of the fabric cutout and the surrounding fabric. This prevents fraying and loose edges. Allow to dry.

For the Hat:

1. Fold back the brim of the hat to the crown near the front. Glue or hand-stitch in place.

2. Glue a silk sunflower to the brim where you folded it back. Allow to dry.

Crackled and Beaded Shirt and Headband

Primary Techniques: Bleaching and Beading

Start With...

Brightly colored cotton T-shirt

And Add...

Fabric Crackle (source: Delta)

Bleach

Pony beads: about 80 silver, about 80 gold (source: The Beadery)

Wood beads: about 80, 9 mm, pink

From Your Craft Cupboard

Scissors **Ruler**

Fabric marker with disappearing ink

Sponge brush

Needle and thread in color to match the T-shirt for hand stitching (for headband)

Sewing machine and notions (for headband)

T-shirt board or aluminum foil or waxed paper

Then Simply...

1. Wash the shirt to remove any sizing; do not use fabric softener. Dry in the dryer. Put the shirt on a T-shirt board or place aluminum foil or waxed paper between the front and the back.

2. Apply Fabric Crackle according to the manufacturer's instructions to the center of the T-shirt, tapering off toward the bottom. Do not apply to the ribbed neckline and the sleeves.

3. Mix ½ cup water and ½ cup bleach. Sponge onto the front of the shirt, over the Crackle. Let dry. Wash Fabric Crackle off, following the manufacturer's instructions; dry.

4. Measure 4" up from the bottom of the T-shirt; mark a straight line across the shirt, and cut the bottom of the shirt off. Save this piece for the headband. Cut the ribbing edge off the sleeves.

5. To fringe the bottom of the shirt and sleeves, cut up from the raw edges 2"; space the cuts about ¼" apart.

6. Slide the beads onto these fringe strips on the shirt bottom and sleeves. First slide on a gold pony bead, then a pink wooden one, then a silver pony bead; push the beads up to the solid part of the shirt and knot the

end of the fringe strip so the beads don't come off. Continue all around the bottom of the shirt and the sleeves.

For the Headband:

1. Cut the loop of fabric you cut off the bottom of the shirt across the 4" width to make a long, narrow strip.

2. Fold the strip in half lengthwise, with the right side in, to form a 2" x about 36" rectangle. Stitch a ¼" seam along the long edge and down one 2" end to the fold. Turn this strip right side out; push the open end into the tube about ¼" and whipstitch closed. Iron flat. Tie the fabric strip around your head, and let the ends hang free.

Label-Pocket Tee

Primary Technique: Gluing

Start With...

Black T-shirt

Pocket cut from denim jeans

And Add...

Labels cut from other clothes

From Your Craft Cupboard

Scissors

Washable fabric glue

T-shirt board or aluminum foil or waxed paper

Then Simply...

1. Carefully cut colorful fabric labels from clothes. Arrange them on the denim pocket at odd angles, overlapping and running off the edges, until you have a pleasing arrangement.

2. Following the gluing instructions on page 9, glue the labels to the pocket one at a time. Start with the ones on the bottom layer, then overlap other labels on them. Where the labels go off the edge, cut them even with the pocket. Allow to dry.

3. Avoid adhering the front of the shirt to the back by using a T-shirt board or placing waxed paper or aluminum foil between the layers. Turn the pocket over, and run a line of glue on the seams around the pocket edge, but not at the top of the pocket. Using the photo as a guide, press the pocket in place on the T-shirt. Allow to dry.

Come to the Fair
Gypsy Vest

Gypsy Vest

Primary Technique: Gluing

Start With...

Black grosgrain vest:
(source: Hirschberg Schutz)

And Add...

Woven ribbons: 1" x 24" each of 3 different patterns

Satin ribbons: about 24" long in varied widths ($3/16$", $1/4$", and $3/8$" shown), in each of 4 different colors

Sew-on coins: about 24, $3/8$"–$1/2$" in diameter, with hole in top for stitching (or use charms)

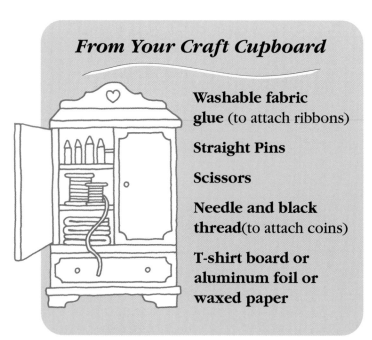

From Your Craft Cupboard

Washable fabric glue (to attach ribbons)

Straight Pins

Scissors

Needle and black thread (to attach coins)

T-shirt board or aluminum foil or waxed paper

Then Simply...

1. Lay the vest, front up, on a smooth work surface. Lay the ribbons vertically on the right side of the vest front, starting with a satin ribbon at the armhole, then alternating the woven and satin ribbons side by side across the front of the vest, using the photo as a guide. Pin in place at the top, middle, and bottom when you have a pleasant arrangement.

2. Trim off the ends of the ribbons where they meet the shoulder seam and the bottom of the vest.

3. Glue the ribbons to the vest, one at a time. Remove the pins from 1 ribbon, apply glue to the back, and press back in place on the vest. Then, glue the next ribbon, until all are glued down. To avoid adhering the front of the vest to the back, use a T-shirt board or place aluminum foil or waxed paper between the layers.

4. Use the needle and black thread to hand-stitch the coins to the left side of the vest, scattering them randomly.

Guatemalan Tote and Matching Shirt

Primary Techniques: Sewing and Fusing
or Gluing

Start With...

Woven Guatemalan serape, table runner, or fabric (about 15" x 45")

Chambray shirt with pockets

And Add...

To Make the Tote:

Woven Guatemalan sash with tassels:
2, each 1½" x 50"; bright color(s) to match
fabric (red and fuchsia shown)

To the Shirt:

Guatemalan fabric (pieces left from
making tote)

Tiny Guatemalan "worry" dolls

Dimensional fabric paint: with fine-line applicator tip, bright color to coordinate with fabric

From Your Craft Cupboard

**Ruler or
measuring tape**

**Sewing machine
and notions**

Scissors

Straight pins

Tracing paper

Pencil

**Fusible webbing or
washable fabric glue**
(to attach fabric shapes)

Iron and pressing cloth or light towel
(if using fusible webbing)

Craft knife (if shirt pocket has snap
or button)

**T-shirt board or aluminum foil or
waxed paper** (if gluing)

Then Simply...

For the Tote:

1. Cut a strip of fabric 15" wide and 36" long.
Hem each 15" end of the fabric strip
separately; fold one end to the back of the

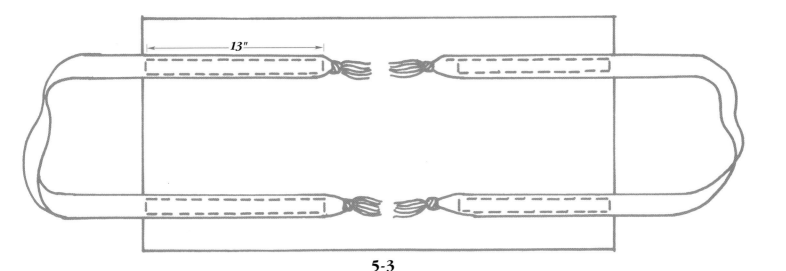

13"

5-3

fabric about ¼", and run a straight stitch near the raw edge. Fold again about 2" more, and straight-stitch again at both the folded edge and the inside edge you previously hemmed. Repeat for the other end.

2. Turn the fabric hemmed side down. Pin 1 of the woven straps to one end of the fabric, as shown in Diagram 5-3. About 13" should overlap the fabric on each end; it should lie parallel to the long edge of the fabric. For strength, stitch down one side of the strap to within about 1" of the end of the strap, across the strap, and up the other side of the strap to the end of the fabric, and across to where you began. Repeat for the second half of the strap.

3. Repeat Step 2 for the strap at the other end of the fabric.

4. Fold the fabric in half, right side in, with the two straps at one end. Straight-stitch down the two sides, as shown in Diagram 5-4, taking about a ¼" seam.

5. Turn the tote so one seam is facing you. Pull the two sides out near the bottom corner to allow you to flatten the tote where the seam meets the bottom fold. Measure 1½" up the seam and run a line of straight stitching at a 90° angle to the seam, as shown in Diagram 5-5. Repeat for the other corner. This stitching allows the bag to stand up more readily when you have things in it.

6. Turn the tote right side out.

For the Shirt:

1. If using fusible webbing, iron it on the back of the fabric, following the fusing instructions on page 9. Turn the fabric right side up.

2. Lay the shirt on a flat work surface. Use tracing paper and a pencil to trace the shapes of 1 pocket and 1 yoke (on opposite sides of the shirt front). To trace the yoke, go across the shoulder seam, down

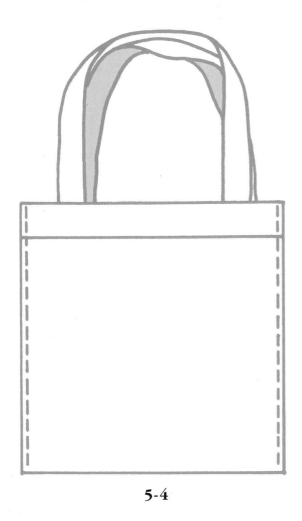

5-4

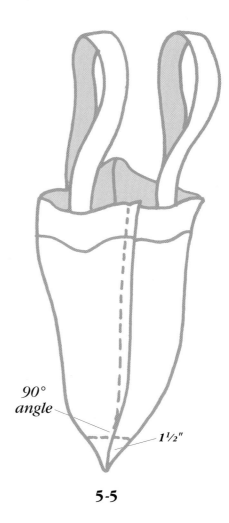

90°
angle

1½"

5-5

the arm opening, across the chest just above the pocket, up the button placket, and around the collar to return to the shoulder seam.

3. Remove the tracing paper and lay the shirt flat on your work surface. Go over the tracing lines of the shapes, using a ruler to straighten them, if needed, and smoothing curved lines.

4. Pin the tracing paper for the pocket and yoke to the print fabric and cut out the shapes.

5. Fuse or glue the fabric in place on the shirt.

6. If the shirt has snaps or buttons on the pocket, use the point of a craft knife to cut through the material where it overlaps the snap or button. Push the fabric down around the snap or just under the edge of the button. Be careful not to cut the fabric of the shirt.

7. Run a thin line of dimensional fabric paint around the fabric shapes where they meet the shirt. Be sure the paint touches both the shirt and the edge of the fabric. This prevents fraying and loose edges. Allow to dry.

8. Stitch the worry dolls to the edge of the pocket flap.

African Ambience

Left: **Safari Tee**
Right: **African Print Shirt**

Safari Tee

Primary Technique: Rubber Stamping

Start With...

White T-shirt

And Add...

Rubber stamps: wild animal motifs, such as giraffe, zebra, jaguar, and cheetah (source: Rubber Stampede)

Stamp pads: with brown and black ink for fabric stamping

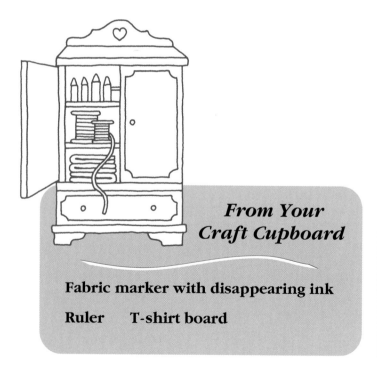

From Your Craft Cupboard

Fabric marker with disappearing ink

Ruler   T-shirt board

Then Simply...

1. Wash the shirt to remove sizing; do not use fabric softener. Air- or machine-dry. Put the shirt on a T-shirt board to hold it while you mark the guidelines and stamp the design.

2. Using a marker with disappearing ink, mark a guideline across the chest, between the armholes; make sure it is straight across the shirt by measuring down from the shoulder seams at the armhole about 7". Mark a second guideline 3" farther down the shirt; mark the third and fourth guidelines, each down another 3".

3. Stamp a row of 4 zebras about 2" apart on the top guideline using black ink. Use brown ink to stamp a row of giraffes on the second line, just below the zebras on the top guideline. Make a row of black jaguars on the third line, and then a row of brown cheetahs on the bottom line.

4. Allow to dry. Clean your rubber stamps.

African Print Shirt

Primary Techniques: Fusing and Gluing

Start With...

Black T-shirt

Bandanna: about 14" square, African Woven Blanket print (source: Marks Handkerchief Manufacturing)

And Add...

Dimensional fabric paint: with fine-point applicator tips, in bright red, yellow, and green (to coordinate with bandanna colors)

Beaded trim: 1½"-long bead strings hung from woven trim, brown and black

Then Simply...

1. If using fusible webbing, iron it on the back of the bandanna, following the fusing instructions on page 9. Turn the bandanna right side up.

2. Fold the bandanna in half, from one corner to the opposite corner, to form 2 triangles (see Diagram 5-6). Cut on the fold. Lay 1 triangle aside.

3. Lay the shirt flat on your work surface, face up. Place the bandanna triangle on the shirt, with the raw edge across the shoulder seams. If the triangle extends past the armhole seam, cut off a row or rows of the design along the finished edges until the bandanna fits between the armhole seams.

From Your Craft Cupboard

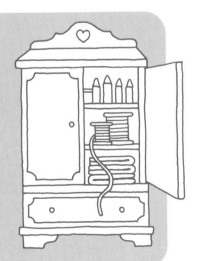

Ruler

Fabric marker with disappearing ink or pencil

Scissors

Fusible webbing or washable fabric glue
(to attach fabric cutouts)

Washable fabric glue (to attach beaded trim)

Iron and pressing cloth or light towel
(if using fusible webbing)

T-shirt board or aluminum foil or waxed paper

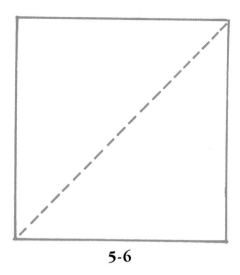

5-6

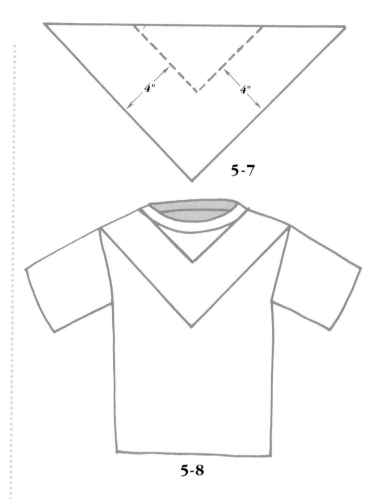

5-7

5-8

4. Measure about 4" up from the bottom edge of the bandanna and cut along the design to form a V shape, using the photo and Diagram 5-7 as guides.

5. Fuse or glue the bandanna to the shirt with the top of the V at the shoulder seams (see Diagram 5-8). If gluing, avoid adhering the front of the shirt to the back by using a T-shirt board or placing waxed paper or aluminum foil between the layers.

6. Cut about 10 rectangles from the remaining bandanna fabric, each about 2" x 3". Fuse or glue them to the shirt below the V-shaped bandanna at odd angles (see the photo).

7. Glue the beaded trim at the bottom edge of the V-shape of the bandanna, covering the raw edge (or rolled hem) of the bandanna. If beaded trim is not available, you can create your own by stitching strings of beads about 1½" long every ¼" along the edge of a black woven trim.

8. Run a thin line of yellow dimensional fabric paint around along the top edge of the V-shaped bandanna fabric and across the shoulder where the raw edge of the bandanna meets the shirt. Run thin lines of red, yellow, and/or green dimensional fabric paint around the rectangles of bandanna fabric on the shirt beneath the V. Be sure the paint touches both the shirt and the edge of the fabric. This prevents fraying and loose edges.

9. Run a zigzag of red dimensional fabric paint on the woven trim at the bottom of the V-shaped bandanna. Also paint a zigzag about ½" wide at the top of the bandanna V.

For the Fun of It

Several just-for-fun projects conclude this book. Kids will love helping out on the Halloween costumes, and the decorated caps are sure to be on any teen's hit parade. For the grown-ups, there are tops and aprons that are as lively as they are practical.

Native American Brave Shirt

Primary Techniques: Sewing and Gluing

Start With...

Tan standard-size pillowcase (or dye a white one tan)

And Add...

Native American- or Southwestern-print trim: 4 yards

Suede-like fringe: 4 yards, brown

Conchos: 4, about 1" diameter, silver

Pony beads: 16, turquoise

Velcro® fastener: beige

Halloween makeup: bright colors

Then Simply...

1. Measure your brave from the shoulder seam to the hip. Cut the pillowcase to that length at the open end. Cut the leftover fabric into 4 strips, each 15" x 1", to be used later to thread through the conchos. Fringe the bottom of the shirt by cutting up from the bottom about 2" every ¼" all around.

2. Fold the pillowcase along the short seamed end to find the center; pin or mark with a fabric marker. Lay the pillowcase flat on your work surface with the right side out. Measure 3½" out from the center mark along the seam in both directions. Draw almost a half circle between these two

From Your Craft Cupboard

Tape measure	Washable fabric glue
Straight pins Scissors	Fabric marker with disappearing ink or pencil
Needle and beige thread for hand stitching	Iron
Sewing machine and notions	Aluminum foil or waxed paper

Costume Capers

Left to right: **Native American Brave, Cowboy Dude,**
Silvery Angel, Glittery Witch

marks to form the neckline; cut out and remove the piece from the pillowcase. Cut 5" straight down the center back of the pillowcase from the neckline.

3. To mark the armholes, lay the pillowcase on your work surface again with the cut neckline up. Start at one corner where the side seam meets the top edge with the neck opening. Measure about 2" in from the corner toward the neckline and mark with a pin or fabric marker; measure down the seamed side edge about 6". Mark and cut a gentle curve between these two points for the armhole; adjust the size of the armhole for smaller or larger children before you cut; look at clothes your little brave wears for a better idea of the correct size. After you have cut one armhole, turn it over and pin it to the opposite corner for a pattern; cut out that armhole. To fringe armholes, make 3"-long cuts every ⅜" around each armhole.

4. Glue some brown suede-like fringe in a V-shape from the shoulder seams on either side of the neckline to the center front of the shirt. Glue some more brown fringe over the pillowcase fringe at the bottom of the shirt. Use the photo as a placement guide. To avoid adhering the front of the shirt to the back, place waxed paper or aluminum foil between the layers.

5. Glue Native American- or Southwestern-print trim at the solid edge of the suedelike fringe.

6. Attach a Velcro® fastener at the top of the neck opening slit.

7. Thread the strips of fabric cut in Step 2 through the conchos and pull the ends so they hang out to the front evenly. Make an overhand knot with the 2 ends to secure the fabric to the conchos. Add 2 pony beads to each of the hanging ends; knot the fabric beneath the beads to keep them from falling off. Stitch the conchos to the shirt: 1 at the center front and 3 across the front of the shirt at the bottom (see the photo).

8. Tie the remaining print trim around the head for a headband. Add elastic if desired for a snug, but comfortable, fit.

To Complete the Costume: Wear the shirt with a pair of brown slacks or jeans and moccasins. Paint your brave's face with Halloween makeup "war paint."

Cowboy Shirt and Chaps

Primary Techniques: Sewing and Fusing

Start With...

Child-size blue chambray shirt

Cow-print fabric: 1 yard

And Add...

To the Chaps:

Grommets: 8, ½" hole (optional)

Fray Check® (if not using grommets)

Rawhide lacing: 1 yard

To the Shirt:

Cow-print fabric: scraps from making chaps

Fringe: about 12", black

Then Simply...

For the Chaps:

1. Measure your little cowpoke's leg length and waist.

2. Cut 2 pieces of cow-print fabric, each 9" x leg length; these are the chaps. Cut another 2 pieces, each 5" wide and as long as the waist measurement; this is the waistband.

From Your Craft Cupboard

Tracing paper

Pencil   Tape measure

Ruler or yardstick

Straight pins   Scissors

Sewing machine and notions

Fusible webbing or washable fabric glue (to attach fabric to shirt)

Washable fabric glue (for fringe)

Aluminum foil or waxed paper

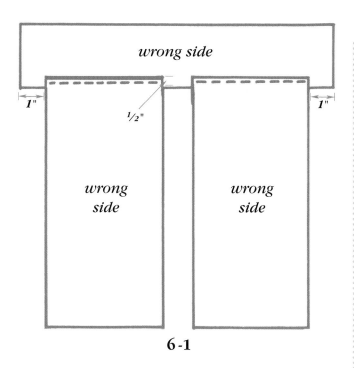

6-1

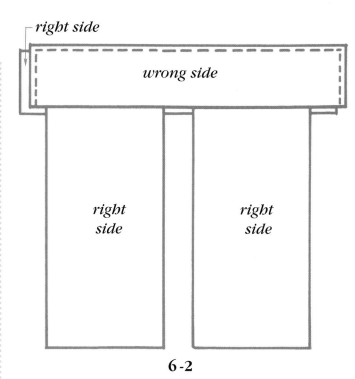

6-2

3. Lay 1 of the waistband pieces face down on your work surface. Lay the 2 pieces for the chaps face down about 1" in from the ends of the waistband; the 9" end of the chaps should overlap the waistband about ¹⁄₂" (see Diagram 6-1). Pin or baste the chaps in place, then stitch them to the waistband.

4. Turn the waistband and chaps piece right side up. Place the other waistband piece directly over the one you just sewed the chaps to, with the right sides of the fabric together. Pin or baste, then sew across one end, along top edge, and across the other end of the waistband (see Diagram 6-2).

5. Turn the waistband right side out. Fold about ¹⁄₄" of the raw edge at the bottom of the waistband to the inside to make a finished edge; pin or baste, then topstitch

along all four sides of the waistband, through both layers of the waistband and the chaps (see Diagram 6-3).

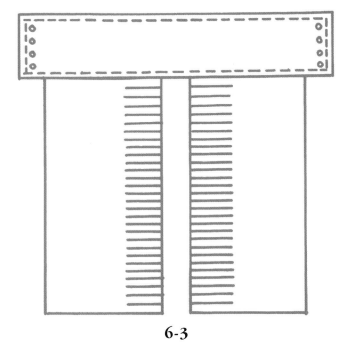

6-3

6. Add 4 grommets to each side of the waistband, as shown in Diagram 6-3. If you do not have grommets, punch ¼" holes in their place, and seal the edges of the holes with Fray Check®.

7. Lay the chaps flat on your work surface. Make 3" horizontal cuts every ⅜" along the inside edges of the chaps to form fringe, as shown in Diagram 6-3.

8. Put the chaps around your cowboy's waist and thread the rawhide strip through the grommet holes in the front, the same way you put laces in shoes. Tie a bow to secure.

For the Shirt:

1. If using fusible webbing, iron it on the back of the cow-print fabric, following the fusing instructions on page 9. Turn the fabric right side up.

2. Lay the shirt on a flat work surface. Use tracing paper and a pencil to trace the shapes of the yoke on each side of the shirt front: go across the shoulder seam, down the arm opening, across the chest just above the pocket, up the button placket, and around the collar to return to the shoulder seam.

3. Remove the tracing paper and lay the shirt flat on your work surface. Go over the tracing lines of the shapes, using a ruler to straighten them, if needed, and smoothing curved lines.

4. Pin the tracing paper to the cow-print fabric and cut out the yoke shapes.

5. Fuse or glue the fabric in place on the shirt. If gluing, avoid adhering the front of the shirt to the back by placing waxed paper or aluminum foil between the layers.

6. Glue on the black fringe to the lower edge of the yokes. Run a thin line of fabric glue around the fabric edge and press the sewn edge of the fringe into it. Allow to dry flat.

To Complete the Costume: Round up jeans, boots, and a cowboy hat.

Silvery Angel

Primary Techniques: Sewing and Gluing

Start With...

White standard-size pillowcase

And Add...

Sequin trim: 4 yards, silver

Lace fabric: 1 yard x 45" wide, white

Velcro® fasteners: white

Purchased wings and halo

From Your Craft Cupboard

Tape measure

Straight pins

Scissors

Needle and white thread for hand stitching

Sewing machine and notions

Fabric marker with disappearing ink or pencil

Jewel glue   Iron

Aluminum foil or waxed paper

Then Simply...

1. Measure your little angel from the shoulder seam to the knee. Cut pillowcase to knee length, if necessary.

2. Fold the pillowcase along the seamed short end to find the center; pin or mark with a fabric marker. Lay the pillowcase flat on your work surface with the right side out. Measure 3½" out from the center mark along the seam in both directions. Draw almost a half circle between these 2 marks to form the neckline; cut out and remove the piece from the pillowcase. Cut 5" straight down the center back of the pillowcase from the neckline.

3. To mark the armholes, lay the pillowcase on your work surface again with the cut neckline up. Start at one corner where the side seam meets the top edge with the neck opening. Measure about 2" in from the corner toward the neckline and mark with a pin or fabric marker; measure down the seamed side edge about 6". Mark and cut a gentle curve between these two points for the armhole; adjust the size of the armhole for smaller or larger children before you cut; look at clothes your angel wears for a better idea of the correct size. After you have cut one armhole, turn it over and pin it to the opposite corner for a pattern; cut out that armhole.

4. Cut the lace fabric into the following sizes (or increase or decrease to fit the child): for neckline: 1 piece, 3¼" x 44"; for armholes: 2 pieces, 2½" x 30"; for hemline: 2 pieces, 9" x 45".

5. Run a gathering stitch along one 44" side of the neckline lace; pull the thread to gather to fit the neck opening. Put the lace inside the neck opening, wrong sides together, with the gathered edge of the lace aligned with the raw edge of the neckline. The opening in the lace should be at the opening in the back of the neckline; pin or baste in place. Stitch the neckline and the lace together with a ¼" seam. Flip the lace out to the right side of the dress; topstitch about ¼" from the neckline all around the opening. Attach a Velcro® closure at the top of the neck opening slit.

6. Fold the raw edges of the armholes in about ¼" and press in place with an iron. Run a gathering stitch along the 30" side of 1 of the armhole lace pieces; pull the thread to gather to fit the armhole. Put the gathered edge of the lace inside the armhole about ¼", so that the folded edge of the armhole overlaps the gathered edge of the lace; the opening in the lace should be under the arm; pin or baste in place, then topstitch the lace to the armhole. Repeat for the other armhole.

7. Overlap the 2 pieces of 9" x 45" lace and seam along the 9" edges to form a long strip. Run a gathering stitch along one long edge; pull the thread to gather to fit the hemline of the dress. Pin the lace strip to the dress with the right sides together and the gathered edge of the lace at the bottom of the hemline. Take a ¼" seam to attach the lace to the hemline. Flip the lace down.

8. Glue silver sequin trim around the bottom of the dress, just above the lace. Glue another piece of sequin trim around the waistline of the dress. Glue about 24" of sequin trim to the waistline at each side of the dress; when the dress is put on, criss-cross these two pieces on the front of the dress and tie at the neck in back. Use the photo as a placement guide. To avoid adhering the front of the dress to the back, place aluminum foil or waxed paper between layers.

To Complete the Costume: Wear the overdress with a white, long-sleeve turtleneck shirt, white tights, and white shoes. Attach wings and halo.

Glittery Witch

Primary Techniques: Sewing and Gluing

Start With...

Black standard-size pillowcase (or dye a white one black)

And Add...

Black netting with gold glitter polka dots: 10" x 16"

Metallic gold ribbon: ³/₄" x 36"

Gold glitter or spray glitter (source: Cascade)

Gold lamé fabric: 6" x 6"

Velcro® fastener: black

Purchased witch hat

Moon and star patterns on page 145

Then Simply...

1. Measure your trick-or-treater from the shoulder seam to the knee. Cut pillowcase to knee length, if necessary.

2. Fold the pillowcase along the seamed short end to find the center; pin or mark with chalk or pencil. Lay the pillowcase flat on your work surface with the right side out. Measure 3¹/₂" out from the center mark along the seam in both directions. Draw almost a half circle between these two marks to form the neckline; cut out and remove the piece from the pillowcase. Cut 5" straight down the center back of the pillowcase from the neckline.

3. To mark the armholes, lay the pillowcase on your work surface again with the cut

From Your Craft Cupboard

Tracing paper

Pencil   Tape measure

Straight pins   Scissors

Needle and black thread for hand sewing

Sewing machine and notions

Chalk or light-colored marking pencil for fabric

Washable fabric glue

Iron

Aluminum foil or waxed paper

neckline up. Start at one corner where the side seam meets the top edge with the neck opening. Measure about 2" in from the corner toward the neckline and mark with a pin or fabric marker; measure down the seamed side edge about 6". Mark and cut a gentle curve between these two points for the armhole; adjust the size of the armhole for smaller or larger children before you cut; look at clothes your witch wears for a better idea of the correct size. After you have cut one armhole, turn it over and pin it to the opposite corner for a pattern; cut out that armhole.

4. Cut the edges of the armhole and hem into points to make them jagged all around (about 3" deep at armhole and 4" deep at hem).

5. Lay the netting flat on your work surface. Cut points 9" deep along the 16" side. With wrong sides together, align the uncut long edge of the netting with the inside edge of the neckline and pin, starting and ending at

the back opening; the netting should be entirely inside the dress. Take a ¼" seam around the neckline. Flip the netting points to the outside like a collar and topstitch ¼" from the edge all around the neckline. Attach a Velcro® closure at the top of the back opening.

6. Glue the gold ribbon to the bottom of the hem of the dress, above the points. To avoid adhering the front of the dress to the back, place aluminum foil or waxed paper between layers.

7. Use tracing paper and a pencil to trace the moon and star patterns below. Pin the patterns to the gold lamé and cut out the shapes. Glue to the front of the witch hat.

8. Spray gold glitter all over the dress and hat.

To Complete the Costume: Wear the overdress with a black, long-sleeved turtleneck shirt, black tights, and black shoes.

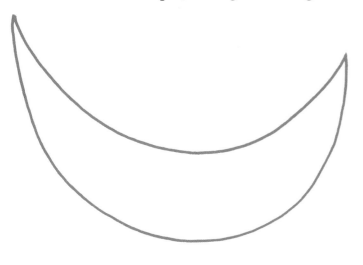

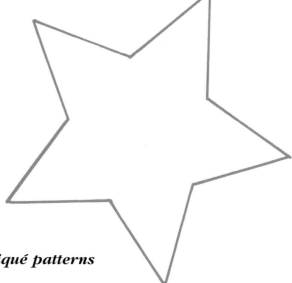

Glittery Witch hat appliqué patterns

Fishy Knit Shirt

Primary Technique: Fabric Painting

Start With...

Dark green knit shirt or other neutral color

And Add...

Fabric paints: Dazzling Metallics pearlized white and pearlized pink; silver, yellow, black, and dark green (source: DecoArt)

Textile extender or medium

Fish painting pattern on page 148

From Your Craft Cupboard

Tracing paper

Graphite paper (use white on a dark shirt; black on a light shirt)

Pencil

Paintrushes: flat and liner

T-shirt board

Then Simply...

1. Trace the fish painting pattern on page 148 using tracing paper and a pencil.

2. Wash the shirt to remove sizing; do not use fabric softener. Air- or machine-dry. Put the shirt on a T-shirt board to hold it while you transfer the design and paint.

3. Place the graphite paper, colored side down, on the shirt where the fish design will be. Put the tracing paper with the fish design over the graphite paper. Use the pencil to retrace the fish design, so it will be transferred to the shirt with the graphite. Remove the graphite and tracing papers.

4. Using the photo as a painting guide and following the instructions on page 11, with a flat brush paint the lower half of the fish and the lower half of the fish head in pearlized white.

5. Using a flat brush, paint the top half of the fish in a dark green.

6. With the pad of your index finger or with a flat brush, pat green paint lightly onto the top of the white area, blending it off into the green at the top half of the fish.

Get Reel

Fishy Knit Shirt

7. Again, with the pad of your index finger or a flat brush, pat pearlized pink paint over the white; allow to dry. Pat on some silver.

8. With a liner brush lightly loaded with silver paint, outline the fish, fins, tail, and face detail.

9. Paint the eye yellow; allow to dry, then dot in a black pupil.

10. With a liner brush, dab in black dots over the fish body.

Sea Sure
Beach Cover-up and Hat

Beach Cover-up and Hat

Primary Techniques: Gold Foiling and Painting

Start With...

Long white T-shirt with cap sleeves
(source: Sunbelt Sportswear)

Straw hat

And Add...

To the Cover-up:

Liquid Beads™ Press and Peel Foil Beginner Kit (source: Plaid Enterprises)

Fabric Paint Matchables: deep turquoise and purple (source: Duncan)

Textile extender or medium

Painting patterns on pages 151 and 152

To the Hat:

Spray sealer

Spray paint: green or turquoise

Satin ribbon: 1" x 2 yards, purple

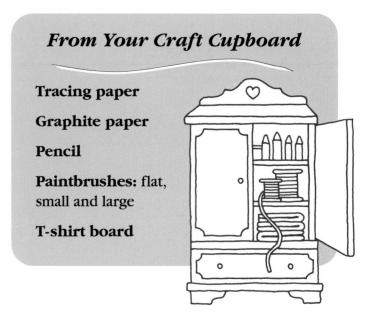

From Your Craft Cupboard

Tracing paper

Graphite paper

Pencil

Paintbrushes: flat, small and large

T-shirt board

Then Simply...

For the Cover-up:

1. Trace the fish painting patterns on pages 151 and 152 using tracing paper and a pencil.

2. Put the shirt on a T-shirt board to hold it while you transfer the designs and paint. Place the graphite paper, colored side down, on the shirt where the fish design will be, using the photo as a guide. Put the tracing paper with the fish design over the graphite paper. Use the pencil to retrace the fish design, so it will be transferred to the shirt with the graphite. Repeat the process for each of the fish. Remove the graphite and tracing papers.

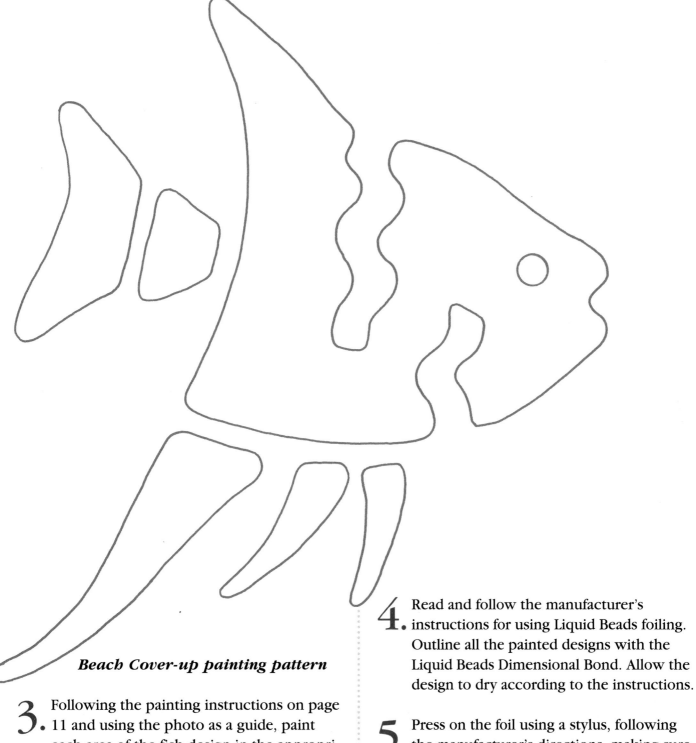

Beach Cover-up painting pattern

3. Following the painting instructions on page 11 and using the photo as a guide, paint each area of the fish design in the appropriate color. Use large brushes to cover bigger areas and small brushes for little areas of the designs. Let the paint dry thoroughly.

4. Read and follow the manufacturer's instructions for using Liquid Beads foiling. Outline all the painted designs with the Liquid Beads Dimensional Bond. Allow the design to dry according to the instructions.

5. Press on the foil using a stylus, following the manufacturer's directions, making sure the foil covers not only the tops but also the sides of the lines you have drawn with the bond. Apply the sealer.

1. Spray the straw hat with sealer to allow better paint coverage. Allow to dry.

2. Spray-paint the sealed straw hat.

3. Glue purple ribbon around the crown of the hat and tie it in a full bow at the back.

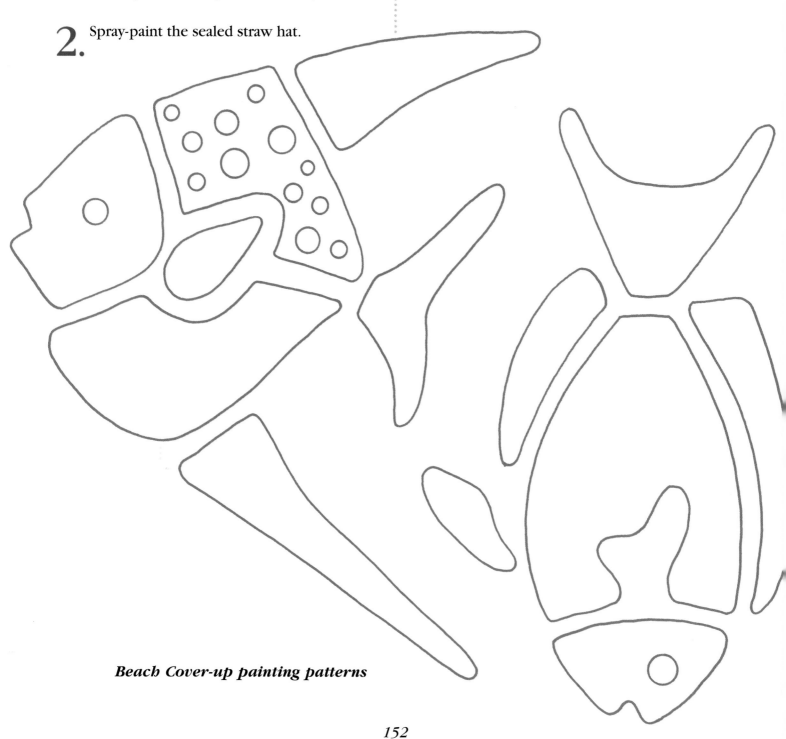

Beach Cover-up painting patterns

Topping It Off
Three Snappy Caps

Three Snappy Caps

Primary Technique: Gluing

Start With...

Red, white, and black baseball-style caps

And Add...

To the Red Cap:

Gingham fabric: about 6" x 12", light green and white

Rickrack: wide, about 28", black

Buttons: about 50, ⅛", black

Dimensional fabric paint: with fine-line applicator tip, light green

To the White Cap:

Doily: 1, round, 5" diameter, white

Rattail cord: ⅛" x 9", burgundy

Pearl string: 9", 3 mm, white

Buttons: 2, ½" and ¾", colors to match roses

Silk roses: 3 small (2 burgundy, 1 rose color)

Charm: about ½" across, goldtone

To the Black Cap:

Lace: 4" x 36", black

String sequins: 3 yards, black

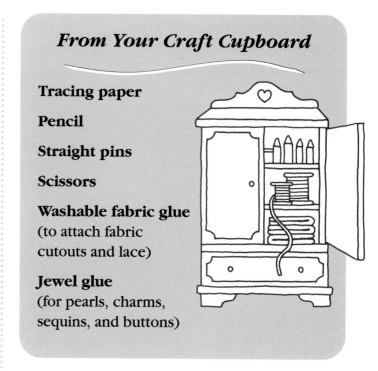

From Your Craft Cupboard

Tracing paper

Pencil

Straight pins

Scissors

Washable fabric glue (to attach fabric cutouts and lace)

Jewel glue (for pearls, charms, sequins, and buttons)

Then Simply...

For the Red Cap:

1. Lay the bill of the cap on the gingham and trace around the outside edge. Cut on that line and a line 1¼" farther in toward the center of the bill. Glue the gingham to the outer edge of the cap.

2. Cut 6 strips of gingham 1¼" x 4". Glue these around the bottom of the crown of the hat, at the base of each of the 6 sections of the cap. Overlap the ends slightly.

3. Glue black rickrack just inside the gingham on the bill of the cap and above the sections of gingham on the crown of the hat, covering one raw edge of the gingham.

4. Run a thin line of green fabric paint around the remaining raw edges where the fabric meets the cap—between the crown and the bill and around the outer edge of the bill. Paint around each of the sections glued onto the cap crown. Be sure the paint touches both the cap and the edge of the fabric. This prevents fraying and loose edges. Allow to dry.

5. Scatter black buttons over all the remaining red areas of the crown and the bill, as if they were melon seeds. Glue in place and allow to dry.

For the White Cap:

1. Cut the round doily in half. Lay the doily on the bill of the cap with the straight cut edge where the bill meets the crown. Glue in place.

2. Glue the rattail cord and the pearl string over the junction where the bill meets the crown.

3. Glue the buttons, roses, and charm over the doily near the junction of the bill and the crown.

For the Black Cap:

1. Use tracing paper and a pencil to trace 1 of the triangular-shaped sections of the hat crown. Pin the tracing to the lace and cut out 6 of these sections.

2. Glue the lace sections to the hat crown.

3. Run a continuous curving, swirling line of glue over the lace, keeping about 1/2" between swirling portions. Press the sequin string into the glue. Do small sections of the hat at a time until it is all covered, using the photo as a guide.

Mr. Fix-It Apron

Primary Technique: Fabric Painting

Start With...

Nail apron

And Add...

Fabric paints: dark green, silver, brown

Textile extender or medium

Washers: 6, flat and tooth styles

Embroidery floss: dark green

Tools painting patterns on pages 158–159

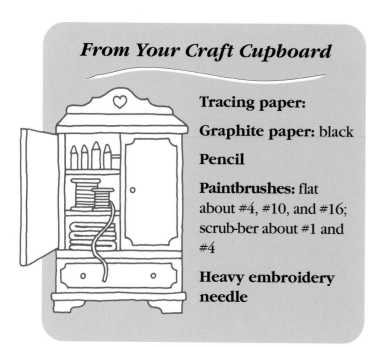

From Your Craft Cupboard

Tracing paper:

Graphite paper: black

Pencil

Paintbrushes: flat about #4, #10, and #16; scrub-ber about #1 and #4

Heavy embroidery needle

Then Simply...

1. Trace the tool painting pattern on pages 158–159 using tracing paper and a pencil. Trace them either as 2 groupings, as they appear, or as individual tool motifs.

2. Put the nail apron on a flat surface. If you wish, you can tape it to the worktable with masking tape or pin it to a piece of corrugated cardboard to hold it while you transfer the designs and paint.

3. Place 2 pieces of graphite paper, black side down, on the apron so they cover the entire pocket area. Put the tracing paper with the tool designs over the graphite paper. Use a pencil to retrace the tool designs, so they will be transferred to the apron with the graphite. Arrange the patterns as shown in the photo or transfer them individually in an arrangement of your choice. Remove the graphite and tracing papers.

4. Following the painting instructions on page 11, paint the tools on the apron, applying the paint much as you would fill in a coloring book design, without shading, using the photo as a color guide. Choose the brushes you are most comfortable with, using flat brushes to fill the large areas of flat color and scrubber brushes to paint smaller areas. Allow to dry.

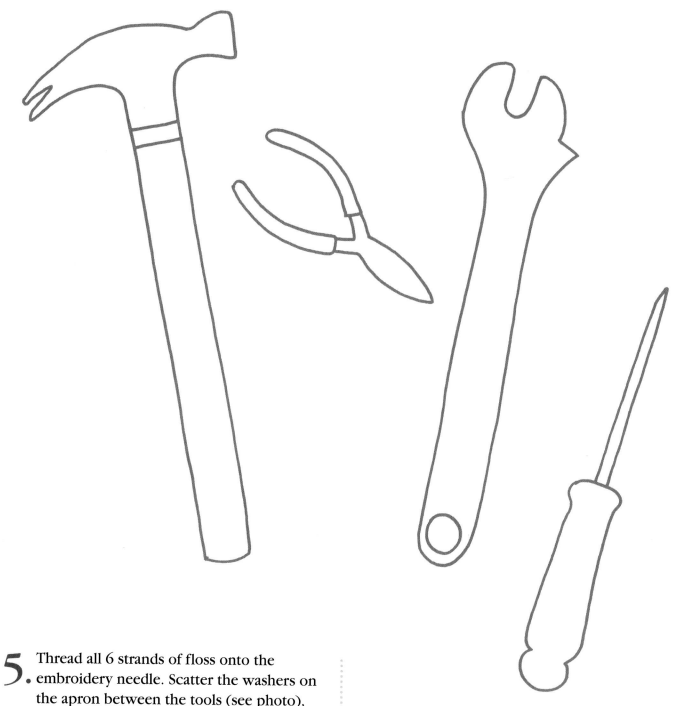

5. Thread all 6 strands of floss onto the embroidery needle. Scatter the washers on the apron between the tools (see photo), and stitch them in place with about 4 stitches in a sunburst pattern, from the inside to the outside of each washer.

Mr. Fix-It Apron painting patterns

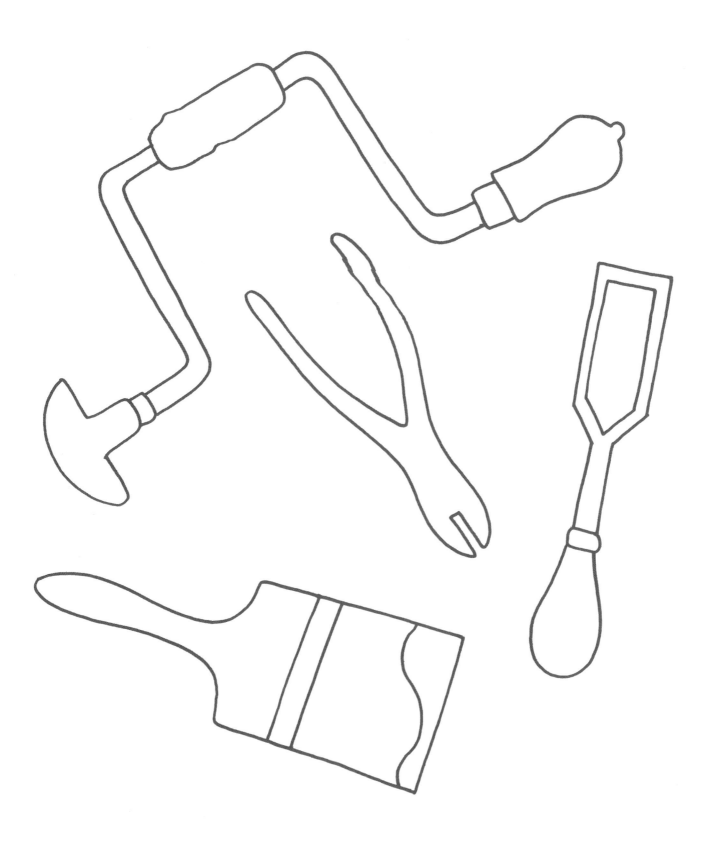

Watermelon Apron

Primary Techniques: Fusing and Hand Sewing

Start With...

Canvas apron in neutral color

And Add...

Checked fabric: 3" x 4", red and cream

Gingham fabric: 6" x 7", red and cream

Dotted fabric: 4" x 5", green and cream

Plaid fabric: 3" x 5", green and cream

Muslin: 4¾" x 5 ½"

Buttons: about 16, ⅛", black

Seed packet pattern, page 163

Then Simply...

1. Use tracing paper and a pencil to trace the individual shapes from the seed packet pattern on page 163. Trace and cut out 2 complete ovals for the piece of watermelon that is partially covered by the second piece—it is easy to continue the pattern lines. Pin the drawings onto the fabrics shown in the photo and cut out the shapes.

2. Hand-stitch the fabrics for the seed packet together, positioning them as shown in the pattern and the photo. First sew the watermelon shapes onto the muslin using straight stitches placed perpendicular to the edge every ¼" around each shape, extending in a sunburst pattern from ⅛" on the fabric to ⅛" on the background.

From Your Craft Cupboard

Tracing paper	Scissors
Pencil	**Needle and heavy black thread for hand stitching**
Graphite paper (optional)	**Fine-line permanent fabric marker**
Ruler Straight pins	

It's the Pits
Watermelon Apron

Stitch the muslin to the red-checked rectangle with a running stitch, then stitch the red-checked rectangle to the apron with a running stitch.

3. Hand-letter WATERMELON and 5¢ on the muslin using a fine-line fabric marker. Add dots at the ends of lines as shown in the pattern and the photo. If you prefer, use tracing paper and graphite paper to transfer the lettering from the seed packet pattern to the muslin rectangle.

4. Scatter the buttons on the apron as if they were seeds pouring from the seed packet. When you achieve an arrangement you like, lift each button individually, make a dot beneath it with the fabric marker, and set it aside; stitch the buttons onto the dots one at a time.

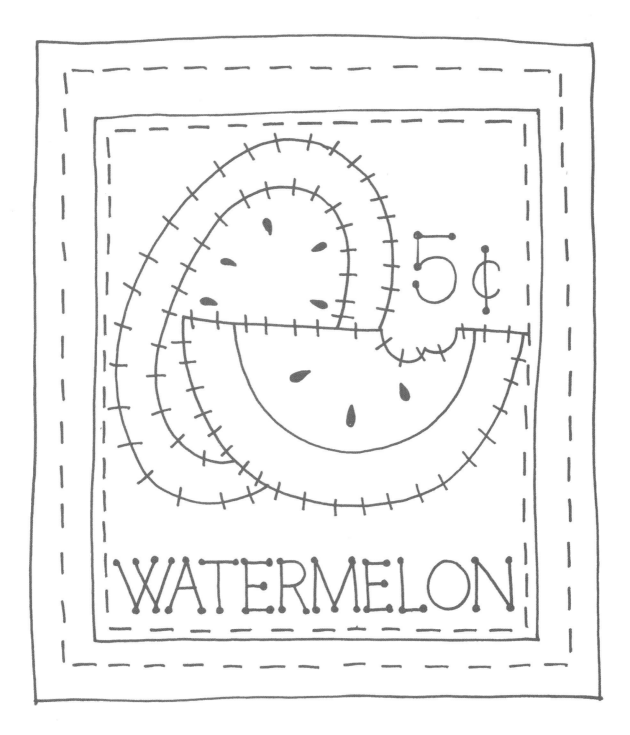

Watermelon Apron seed packet pattern

163

Acknowledgments

BANAR DESIGNS would like to thank all the generous people who allowed us to photograph in their homes and businesses: John and Linda Schmidt, The Grand Tradition, Thee Last Straw, and The Fallbrook Tennis Club.

We want to extend our appreciation to the businesses that provided a special contribution to the formal wear projects: VIP Formal Wear, Carlsbad, CA, for the tuxedo, and Primrose Lane Florist, Fallbrook, CA, for the corsages and boutonniere.

We particularly want to acknowledge the following representatives of companies for their outstanding cooperation: Nancy Overton, Peking Handicrafts; Jeannie Laster, Sunbelt Sportswear; and Susan Jones, Jones Tones Paints.

Sources for Craft Materials

*Contact the following manufacturers to find local sources
for the products used in this book.*

Bandanna, African Style

Marks Handkerchief
Manufacturing Co., Inc.
P.O. Box 2226
Augusta, GA 30903

Bugle Beads

Mill Hill Glass Beads
c/o Gay Bowles Sales
P.O. Box 1060
Janesville, WI 53547

Charms, Coins, and Conchos

Creative Beginnings
475 Morro Bay Boulevard
Morro Bay, CA 93442

Crackle

Delta
2550 Pellissier Place
Whittier, CA 90601

Dye Ties™

Distlefink
P.O. Box 358
Pelham, NY 10803

Fabric Glue, Washable

Unique Stitch™
W. H. Collins
21 Leslie Court
Whippany, NY 07981

Foiling

Jones Tones
68703 Perez Road, D-16/17
Cathedral City, CA 92234

Plaid Enterprises
1649 International Blvd.
Norcross, GA 30091

Fusible Webbing

Wonder-Under®
Pellon Division,
Freudenberg Nonwoven
119 West 40th Street
New York, NY 10018

Hot Stitch Fusible Web
Aleene's
85 Industrial Way
Buellton, CA 93427

Therm O Web/Heat N Bond
112 West Carpenter Avenue
Wheeling, IL 60090

Glitter

Spray Glitter
Cascade Sales and Manufacturing
1352 East Edinger Avenue
Santa Ana, CA 92707

Halogen Glitter
Mark Enterprises
P.O. Box 3094
Newport Beach, CA 92663

Jewel Glue

Gem Tack
Beacon Chemical
275 Sycamore Court, Suite 101
Wyckoff, NJ 07481

**Jewels, Gems, Rhinestones,
and Pony Beads**

The Beadery
P.O. Box 178
Hope Valley, RI 01832

**Laces and Linens: Table Runners,
Handkerchiefs, Doilies, Cutwork
Guest Towels, Battenberg Lace**

Peking Handicrafts
1388 San Mateo Avenue
South San Francisco, CA 94080

Paint, Acrylic

DecoArt
Highway 150 and 27
Stanford, KY 40485

Paint, Dimensional

Delta
2550 Pellissier Place
Whittier, CA 90601

Duncan
5973 East Shields Avenue
Fresno, CA 93727

Jones Tones
68703 Perez Road, D-16/17
Cathedral City, CA 92234

Tulip
24 Prime Parkway
Natick, MA 01760

Paint, Spray Webbing

Carnival Arts
P.O. Box 4656
Scottsdale, AZ 85261

Ribbons and Trims

Wm. E. Wright
South Street
West Warren, MA 01092

**Rubber Stamps, Ink,
and Stamp Pads**

Rubber Stampede
Box 246
Berkeley, CA 94710

**Shirts, Jackets, Dresses,
Tuxedo Shirt, Cap-Sleeve Dress,
Denim Jackets, Chambray
Shirts, T-shirts, etc.**

Sunbelt Sportswear
P.O. Box 791967
San Antonio, TX 78279

Transfer Pens

Sulky of America
3113 Broadpoint Drive
Harbor Heights, FL 33983

Vest and Tie

Hirschberg Schutz & Co. Inc.
565 Green Lane
Union, NJ 07083

Index

All of us at Meredith® Press welcome your questions and comments, so that we may continue to bring you the best crafts books possible. Please address your correspondence to: Customer Service Dept., Meredith Press, 150 East 52nd Street, New York, NY 10022. For additional copies of this or any of our books, call 1-800-679-2803, or visit your local crafts or book stores.